HOPE
FOR A FATHERLESS
GENERATION

DOUG STRINGER

HOPE
FOR A FATHERLESS
GENERATION

Rebuilding Our Foundations

DESTINY IMAGE® PUBLISHERS, INC.

P.O. Box 310, Shippensburg, PA 17257-0310

"Speaking to the Purposes of God for This Generation and for the Generations to Come."

This book and all other Destiny Image, Revival Press, MercyPlace, Fresh Bread, Destiny Image Fiction, and Treasure House books are available at Christian bookstores and distributors worldwide.

For a U.S. bookstore nearest you, call 1-800-722-6774.
For more information on foreign distributors, call 717-532-3040.
Reach us on the Internet: www.destinyimage.com.

ISBN 10: 0-7684-2822-X
ISBN 13: 978-0-7684-2822-3
Previous ISBN 1-56043-139-3

For Worldwide Distribution, Printed in the U.S.A.

1 2 3 4 5 6 7 8 9 10 11 / 13 12 11 10 09

DEDICATION

First of all I want to dedicate this book to all who labor with me. Many have stood with me to reach out to this orphaned generation and made numerous sacrifices in their own lives in order to adopt different spiritual orphans of this generation. Second, I want to dedicate this book to all those sons and daughters in the Lord birthed through this ministry. I'm so very proud of them, and I pray that they too will go on to raise up children in the Lord. May they do greater things for the Gospel than I could ever imagine.

I have since had the privilege of developing a dear friendship with Leonard Ravenhill's son, David, who wrote this poem and read it at his father's funeral. May the same be said of us:

I knew a man who gave his life to see revival fire
He prayed by day, he prayed by night to birth this
one desire

He had but one obsession, to see a glorious bride
Arrayed in spotless purity, brought to her bride-
groom's side.

His power, while in the pulpit, was matched by
very few.

And yet, he loved the closet—there with the God
he knew.

While others strove for man's applause, for
fortune and for fame, He had but one ambition,
to exalt his Master's name.

For eighty-seven years he lived—just for eternity,
a man of faith and wisdom and true humility.
He knew one day he'd have to stand before God's
judgment seat.

And so he ran to win the prize, his mission to
complete. The fortune that he left behind was not
in stocks or gold, but lives transformed and chal-
lenged, their stories yet untold.

Life has no greater privilege than this that I have had, of knowing this great man of God, and having him as "Dad."

DAVID RAVENHILL
(Son of Leonard Ravenhill)

Leonard Ravenhill left a legacy behind him. May we likewise leave a legacy to this generation.

ENDORSEMENTS

Through his knowledge of God and his life experiences, Doug Stringer reveals in layman's terms that the order of God is reestablished through fathers. *Hope for the Fatherless Generation* gives both information and solutions to the world's challenges—starting inside out from your home. It is required reading for all the men of my congregation, and it blesses the women as well.

BISHOP EDDIE L. LONG
Senior Pastor, New Birth Missionary Baptist Church

Doug Stringer has an awesome ministry that is timely, not only for this generation, but also for the coming one. He has challenged and influenced my life.

A.C. GREEN
Former Professional Basketball Player

Doug's book has truly confirmed what I have been feeling in my spirit concerning this nation and its problems. The facts and statistics are astounding. It's a must-read for all American fathers and fathers-to-be.

KEVIN BASS
Former Professional Basketball Player

CONTENTS

PREFACE

When I wrote the first edition of this book in the mid-1990s, under the previous title of *The Fatherless Generation,* I felt a strong urging of the Holy Spirit to issue a prophetic warning to the Church about the perilous situation facing our nation's youth. Fatherlessness in America was at record levels, and there was a generation of young people looking for substance and for direction—in short, for something real to hang on to.

Fourteen years later, I know two things about the book we first released, and these two things are the reasons we determined to release a second edition of the manuscript. The first thing is how vitally important the book's message was, and in fact, still *is*. In the years since it was first released, I have received an overwhelming response from young people, parents, and leaders who shared with me how much the book impacted them. They told me how my message had answered a cry within their own hearts and given them vision for building a better future.

The second thing I know now about the book is how prophetic it truly was. What was true in the early 1990s about the erosion of our moral foundations holds even truer today. As of 2007, nearly a quarter of all children in the United States were growing up without a father in the home, and in certain segments of the population, that number is more than doubled.[1] The studies are conclusive—children fare best in two-parent homes, with both mother and father. This is a truth that we in the body of Christ have always known; and yet, on our watch, the statistics have continued to rise.

Overall, the deterioration of the family and of our nation's Judeo-Christian values is worse than the situation I described in the first edition of *The Fatherless Generation*. Pornography's prevalence on the Internet, movies, and television is more rampant than ever, and the acceptance of homosexuality as a lifestyle is at its highest point. Abortion, euthanasia, adultery, fornication—such practices are not only tolerated in our culture, but in many cases even celebrated and glorified. Is it any wonder that the emerging generation is in peril?

The importance and relevancy of the book's prophetic message—that we must return to the strong foundations of the past lest this generation be swept away by the storms of life—combined with the many requests I received to republish, are what inspired me to release a new edition of *The Fatherless Generation*. The hope of this generation does not lie with shifting philosophical fads, counterfeit religions, or the governments of men. The hope of this generation lies upon the foundation of Christ alone. That is the message of this book and one that I pray will be proclaimed loudly throughout our nation.

For the second edition, we have added a new introductory chapter, as well as a new concluding chapter. Changes to the main portion of text have been kept at a minimum, retaining the original statistics from more than a decade ago in an attempt to highlight how much things have changed since that time—in some cases for the better, in many cases for the worse. And while we did remove some material that has lost its relevancy, we have tried to keep deletions and changes to a minimum.

The generation of youth described in the book is older now,

but I believe that the original manuscript contains important truths that will help us to understand both the previous generation of youth (those who have been known as Generation X) and those who come after them ("Gen Y"). Generation X are adults now, in many cases replacing their retiring parents—the Baby Boomer generation—as leaders in business, government, media, and the Church. What does it mean for a nation to have a fatherless generation at its helm? Moreover, what does it mean for one fatherless generation to lead another? These are questions we must consider as we seek to restore our nation to its biblical and righteous foundations.

In short, this book is for two successive fatherless generations and for those of us in an older generation who still care about the direction we are heading. How do we build on a strong foundation so that we are not swept away by the storms that will come? How do we help the emerging generation reach their full prophetic potential?

The answers to these questions lie with one Person, whose name, Scripture tells us, is called "Everlasting Father" (see Isa. 9:6). It is on the rock foundation of Jesus Christ that we must be established. It is on the principles of His Word that our nation must make its stand. He alone is the hope of the fatherless generation.

I will not leave you as orphans; I will come to you
(John 14:18).

Endnote

1. U.S. Census Bureau Population Survey (2007), http://www.census.gov/compendia/statab/tables/09s0068.pdf (accessed December 31, 2008).

PREFACE TO
THE FIRST EDITION

Where's the beef? Give me something to believe in; I still haven't found what I'm looking for. This is what many in our fatherless, no-direction generation are crying out. A lack of hope and purpose has left many looking for temporary fixes to cover up their fears and insecurities. Without vision and hope, discouragement and compromise settle in. Hopelessness then leads to lawlessness. Proverbs itself tells us that "hope deferred makes the heart sick" (Prov. 13:12a).

An absence of godly leadership and an unwillingness to embrace God as our true leader and heavenly Father have orphaned an entire generation, leaving it with a serious identity crisis.

When I first began to share this message about the no-direction, fatherless generation in 1991, little did I realize how this topic would progress even in America. Today government officials take part in seminars addressing the state of "fatherless America." You see, God always speaks to His Church first, and then His point permeates throughout society as chains of events unfold. The difference here is, society approaches the fatherless generation with a solution that leaves God out. The only solution that will help this generation is one that puts God the Father back into our society and our individual lives.

I do not intend for this book to be a how-to book on fathering. Instead, it examines some of the root causes of the current upheaval that has shaken the fabric of today's society.

How can a generation of orphans understand the love of the heavenly Father when they have no understanding of godly, earthly fathers and mothers? I saw a cartoon by Jim Borgman that depicted some children asking the question, "Mommy, where do daddies come from?"[1] We must adopt this orphaned generation and direct them toward our heavenly Father who desires to seal them all with His Spirit of adoption.

> *For He established a testimony in Jacob, and appointed a law in Israel, which He commanded our fathers, that they should make them known to their children;* **that the generation to come might know them,** *the children who would be born, that they may arise and declare them to their children,* **that they may set their hope in God,** *and not forget the works of God, but keep His commandments;* **and may not be like their fathers, a stubborn and rebellious generation, a generation that did not set its heart aright, and whose spirit was not faithful to God** (Psalm 78:5-8).

Where are the spiritual fathers? The apostle Paul said, "For though you might have ten thousand instructors in Christ, yet you do not have many fathers; for in Christ Jesus I have begotten you through the gospel" (1 Cor. 4:15). We too live in a day with thousands of professional preachers and teachers who are wonderful communicators and orators. Yet where are those who are willing to adopt this orphaned generation? Where are the spiritual parents and disciplers?

> *Give ear, O my people, to my law; incline your ears to the words of my mouth. I will open my mouth in a parable; I will utter dark sayings of old, which we have heard and known, and our fathers have told us.* **We will not hide them from their children, telling to the generation to come the praises of the Lord, and His strength and His wonderful works that He has done** (Psalm 78:1-4).

We need not be bound by the mistakes and consequences of the past decades. We can adopt this present generation who are spiritual orphans and lead them to the Father above. He is a Father to the fatherless and a Husband to the widowed. This generation needs God's intervention!

The Responsibility of Men

Pastor Jack Hayford writes, "In most of His workings, God starts with men."[2] I am in no way suggesting that men are superior to women. Neither am I hinting at any rejection or reduction of the value of women in God's Kingdom purposes.

My heart's desire is that many will be challenged to take their rightful responsibility in their personal lives and families to set an example to this fatherless generation of what godly parents, godly fathers, are all about.

This requires a radical commitment, however—a commitment based on a cause worth dying for. As Dr. Martin Luther King, Jr., once said, "Unless a man finds something worth dying for, he's just as good as dead already." Do we believe the cause of Jesus Christ to be worth dying for?

Therefore, I am issuing a challenge to God's people: be prepared to change. Get a clear vision of all God wants to do. Let His Word live in you. Commit your life to Him without reservation. Lead by serving, and serve by leading. Build up your relationship with Him and with others. Become an ambassador of the King.

> *Have I not commanded you? Be strong and of good courage; do not be afraid, nor be dismayed, for the Lord your God is with you wherever you go* (Joshua 1:9).

> *All that you command us we will do, and wherever you send us we will go* (Joshua 1:16).

> *...The people who know their God shall be strong, and carry out great exploits* (Daniel 11:32).

Genuine passion for God allows no room for mediocrity. It's what we do behind closed doors that determines the power of God—or lack of it—in public.

Let's challenge this present generation to turn their hearts back to God, that they may not be bound by the mistakes of the previous generations. We must reach this generation in order for the next generation and its children to have the praises of the Lord on their lips.

We cannot change our past, but the way we respond to today can bring change for the future.

> *Give ear, O my people, to my law; incline your ears to the words of my mouth. I will open my mouth in a parable; I will utter dark sayings of old, which we have heard and known, and our fathers have told us. We will not hide them from their children, telling to the generation to come the praises of the Lord, and His strength and His wonderful works that He has done. For He established a testimony in Jacob, and appointed a law in Israel, which He commanded our fathers, that they should make them known to their children; that the generation to come might know them, the children who would be born, that they may arise and declare them to their children, that they may set their hope in God, and not forget the works of God, but keep His commandments; and may not be like their fathers, a stubborn and rebellious generation, a generation that did not set its heart aright, and whose spirit was not faithful to God* (Psalm 78:1-8).

Endnotes

1. Jim Borgman, *Cincinnati Enquirer* (King Features, November 1994).

2.   Jack Hayford, "New Orders," *Men of Integrity.Net*, http://www.christianitytoday.com/moi/2005/003/june/28.28.html (accessed December 31, 2008).

Faulty Foundations and Shifting Sands

And the rain fell, and the floods came, and the winds blew and slammed against that house; and yet it did not fall... (Matthew 7:25 NASB).

In early September of 2008, Hurricane Ike slammed into the Texas Gulf Coast, flooding coastal communities, nearly wiping out Galveston Island, and devastating the entire Houston area. The nation's fourth-largest metropolis was paralyzed as millions of people were without power following the storm, many of whom would wait weeks for it to be restored. Our own Somebody Cares offices sustained significant damages, and the ministry was forced to relocate its headquarters while at the same time coordinating relief efforts throughout the region.

Following the storm, images of homes and businesses along the coast flashed over television screens and on Internet news sources. The force of the winds and the water was too much for many of the structures to withstand, and many had been completely destroyed and reduced to mounds of debris that the waves deposited on shore.

In Matthew 7:24-27, Jesus said,

> *Therefore everyone who hears these words of Mine and puts them into practice is like a wise man who built his house on the rock. The rain came down, the streams rose, and the winds blew and beat against that house; yet it did not fall, because it had its foundation on the rock. But everyone who hears these words of Mine and does not put them into practice is like a foolish man who built his house on sand. The rain came down, the streams rose, and the winds blew and beat against that house, and it fell with a great crash* (NIV).

The principle to be learned in this parable is that without the right foundation, a structure cannot stand. If you build on the sand, which shifts and washes away when the storms rise, your house will not stand. It is only upon a solid foundation that a house can stand. And it is only upon a solid foundation that a person, a family, or a nation can be secure.

Since the dawn of civilization, family has been the cornerstone and foundation on which all things were built. But over the years, we have watched the family structure unravel to the point where legislators and judges redefine the meaning of *family* and *marriage*. Fatherlessness abounds. Divorce rates are skyrocketing. *Alternative lifestyles* are becoming normalized. What was once a solid foundation in this nation has now shifted, and as a result, our culture lies in great danger for the storms ahead.

A Prophetic Warning

In the days leading up to Hurricane Ike, local officials warned residents along Texas's southeast Gulf Coast of the magnitude of the storm that was coming. Mandatory evacuation orders were issued for coastal communities, and many residents heeded the warnings and fled inland. Many did not.

Thinking that they could ride out the storm, individuals and even entire families decided to stay in their homes near the rising waters. The day before Ike made landfall, the storm surge began rising significantly and many areas began flooding hours before the storm even hit! This early flooding may have proved to be the mercy of God, as in many cases, rescuers were able to be deployed and airlift people who were already trapped by the rising waters. As a result, they were taken to safety prior to the storm making landfall. But many did not get out before Ike hit and they lost everything, some even their very lives.

When we published *The Fatherless Generation* for the first time in 1994, I knew the book was a prophetic warning. Like many other leaders in the Body of Christ who began issuing wake-up calls to the Church, I could see the writing on the wall. A generation was in crisis, growing up without fathers, resulting in a massive destabilization of our society. Ministries like Promise Keepers and Christian Men's Network, along with many other churches and leaders, focused on building strong husbands and fathers. Many men were rescued, saving entire families and transferring them to "safer ground" on which they would have refuge from the storm.

But just like with Hurricane Ike, many have ignored the warnings. Our nation is battered by winds and waves that continue to erode our moral foundation, and today a whole new generation is emerging without foundations and without fathers. They are a generation on shifting sand, and our national *house* is in danger of falling. When the storms come—be it economic storms, spiritual storms, or natural disasters—the structure will come tumbling down.

An Issue of the Heart

Several years ago, while attending the Congressional Presidential Prayer Breakfast in Washington, D.C., I was honored and humbled to participate in the taping of two television specials on "The Soul of America" with the late Dr. Bill Bright, Chuck Colson of Prison Fellowship, and Max Lucado. As we spoke, I realized that you cannot change the soul of a person, a family, a community, or a nation if the heart is sick. In America, the heart of our nation is the Church.

When King Josiah recognized in Second Kings 22 that everything was out of order, he reinstated the Law for people to follow, which is a good thing and the right thing to do. But unless we follow the Lord's commands with our hearts, not merely paying lip service, we will not see lasting change.

For example, several years ago I was co-facilitating a gathering at the Billy Graham Training Center in North Carolina on the same day that the U.S. Senate failed to pass the Marriage and Family Act Amendment. I was contacted by a Houston radio program that wanted to get my views in a live interview that evening. During the program, they asked me this question: "When the majority of our U.S. Senate say they go to church and claim to be Christians, how can their voting be so blatantly at the opposite end of the spectrum of beliefs?" My reply was, "That's the difference between serving an institutional Christianity and pursuing a relationship with the living Christ."

Our nation has institutions and foundations that are cracked. But we cannot make lasting change unless we, the Church, first deal with our root issues of the heart. Changing laws cannot change hearts, but once hearts are changed, the laws will naturally and progressively change.

Divine Rescue

When a person has a heart attack or for some other reason the heart stops beating, emergency workers will first use hands-on massage to manually "jump-start" the heart. If that doesn't work, the next step is to use a defibrillator, which sends an electronic jolt to the heart in an effort to revive it so it can beat freely once again.

Because of the cracks in our foundation, we—like a weakened heart—are on the verge of collapse. God has been giving us a wake-up call, but we have been pushing our snooze buttons. He has been trying to massage our hearts back to being pliable in His hands and to having life again.

This is the nature of God—to rescue and to save. Like the early efforts of rescuers in the hours before Hurricane Ike, God wants to reach us *before* calamity strikes. Perhaps we have not heeded the warnings before, but if we call out for help while there is still time, will He not come down and *airlift* us to safety? Psalm 50:15 says, "Call upon Me in the day of trouble; I shall rescue you, and you will honor Me" (NASB).

Building an Ark of Refuge

The Bible equates the wickedness of the last days to the days of Noah. It says in Luke 17:26-27,

> *And just as it happened in the days of Noah, so it will be also in the days of the Son of Man: they were eating, they were drinking, they were marrying, they were being given in marriage, until the day that Noah entered the ark, and the flood came and destroyed them all* (NASB).

Before the floods came, however, God instructed Noah how to build an ark of refuge that would preserve the future generation. In the same way, God desires for His Church to be an ark of refuge for the fatherless generation, rescuing them from the consequences of an immoral, rebellious society that has left them stranded in a house built on shifting sands. But like Noah, we must build according to God's instructions so that the refuge can withstand the storm.

God gave Noah a very detailed building plan. Noah had no idea what to expect from the floods. Noah had no idea how long their boat trip would last—much longer than a three-hour tour! Noah had no idea how to house all the animals and keep his family safe from the storms. Noah didn't know, but God knew.

God's building plans are specific. And they are perfect.

> *The law of the Lord is perfect, restoring the soul; the testimony of the Lord is sure, making wise the simple. The precepts of the Lord are right,*

*rejoicing the heart; the commandment of the
Lord is pure, enlightening the eyes. The fear of
the Lord is clean, enduring forever; the judg-
ments of the Lord are true; they are righteous
altogether. They are more desirable than gold,
yes, than much fine gold; sweeter also than honey
and the drippings of the honeycomb. Moreover,
by them Your servant is warned; in keeping them
there is great reward* (Psalm 19:7-11).

When we follow God's pattern, as set forth in His Word, we
are safe from the storm. When we obey His law, the soul of our
culture will be restored. When we heed His testimony, we will have
wisdom on how to govern our nation, our cities, and our homes.
God's pattern is perfect, and there is great reward in following it.
But when we abandon His ways, there is only calamity ahead.

God's Pattern: Relationship

God's pattern for redemption has always been the same: relationship. A vibrant, intimate, personal relationship with our
heavenly Father is our refuge from the storm and the key to abundant life and peace. And as the people of God, our responsibility
is to demonstrate this kind of relationship to a lost and hurting
world.

John 1:14 says, "The Word became flesh and dwelt among
us." God's blueprint for rescuing mankind was the incarnational
ministry of Jesus Christ. But we in the Church have substituted
relationship with programs. Dr. Richard Halverson, the former
chaplain of the U.S. Senate, has said:

> Christianity began in the land of Palestine with the person of Jesus. It went to Greece and became a philosophy, went to Rome and became an institution, went to Western Europe and became a culture. Then it came to America and became an enterprise.

We have digressed in our churches to organization instead of relationship, to marketing God instead of presenting His Gospel, and to institutionalized religion instead of the impartation of life.

What a generation without fathers needs more than anything is a Church that will demonstrate the true nature and character of God to those who are lost and hurting, that will show them that He is a Father who loves them and wants nothing more than to be with them in order that they might know Him and be known of Him. This is the pattern that we should be following.

Out of Alignment

How is it that we as a Church have gone off course so much? How is it that we have substituted programs and dead religion for the extravagant love relationship that God the Father offers those who receive His Son? The truth is, it is easy to go off course a little at a time, and before long, you are far from your desired path. And when a foundation is cracked or built incorrectly, it is easy for the rest of the house to be out of order and not aligned properly.

I learned this principle firsthand once from my mom. I was leaving the house one day to minister when she stopped me.

"Dougie!" she said with her strong Japanese accent, pointing out that the walls of the house were beginning to crack because the foundation was shifting. "If foundation not fixed, everything else will go bad!" I didn't want to listen at the time because I was trying to focus on the message I had been preparing and on other ministry trips that were coming up. But as usual, Mother was right! We later had to fix the walls, the plumbing, and other things all because the foundation was neglected!

I have also seen this lesson in action when I go to the chiropractor. At times I have problems with my knee. My knee problems cause my hip to fall out of place, and pretty soon I feel chronic pain in my back. At that point, I need to go in for an alignment! When I get my spine back in alignment, everything else feels better.

Hope for the Fatherless Generation

By returning to the right foundation, we will be properly aligned and ready to build a place of refuge for the next generation. Many are in the valley of decision and crying out for something real to believe in. There is a lost and hurting generation who needs to see the incarnational ministry of Jesus Christ once again. They aren't interested in programs or hype or the type of Church they've seen in the past—filled with compromise, scandal, and hypocrisy. They need to see a Church that manifests the nature of the One who is a Father to the fatherless. He is their hope. We are their hope.

Leeland and Jack Mooring say it so well in their song, *Tears of the Saints*, that I get tears in my eyes every time I listen to it. They sing of the prodigal sons, the broken and needy, and how tears of the saints are being shed over the emergency of our times. "Father, we will lead them home," the song says.

May this be our commitment to this generation. *Father, we **will** lead them home!*

CHAPTER 1

The No-Direction Generation

An almost perfect relationship with his father was the earthly root of all his wisdom. From his own father, he said, he first learned that Fatherhood must be at the core of the universe. He was thus prepared in an unusual way to teach that religion in which the relation of the Father and Son is of all relations the most central.

—C.S. LEWIS (referring to George MacDonald)

America's streets are filled with people begging, getting high, stealing, and selling—whether it's drugs, stolen merchandise, someone's body, or their own. There are the indigent, the homeless, and the transient. Alcoholics, bums, addicts, AIDS carriers, the unemployed, the unskilled, and the uneducated—all overflow the streets.

But they are not the only ones. There are the children: runaways, the middle class, teenagers. They're confused, lost, unmotivated, unwanted, unloved, and afraid.

After years of ministering to nameless hordes in city streets around the world, the condition, concerns, and confusion of the present American generation has led me to call them the "no-direction" generation. They are a generation without fathers, which is a first for America. Sixty percent of American young people are now raised without a father in the home. In some communities of the American population, babies have only a one-in-five chance to grow to age 16 with two parents in the home.

The baby boomers and the self-centered *me generation* of the 1960s and 1970s have birthed a generation that feels largely unneeded and unwanted. The previous generation, programmed *to tune in, turn on, and drop out,* found marriage confining and parenting restrictive. The fathers tended to bail out, leaving the mothers to shoulder a load of resentment in trying to be two parents instead of one. The mothers' resulting identity crisis was not resolved in time to solve the identity crises of the children.

A rapidly rising men's movement, pioneered by the Church and emulated by the world, aimed to bring dads home to roost. Yet, for hundreds of thousands, it is too late. Adulthood has caught them without a man in the house. For them, the Church must begin with basic fathering. Not knowing what fatherhood is, this generation winces at discipline, scorns correction, and shrinks at defeat. They need to learn from us, the Church, that God is the Father to the fatherless.

America, Our Nation

What kind of life do we promise our children? Homosexuality is taught as an acceptable alternative in public schools nationwide. Drug abuse, violent crimes, and pornography have reached an all-time high, while the value of human life has hit an all-time low with killing for sport, demands for abortion, suicide rights, and euthanasia. Gangs are destroying neighborhoods. Adultery and fornication are viewed by television producers as normal and by the Church as common—even in the clergy.

Our nation was founded on the basis of religious freedom. At one time America sent out 90 percent of all missionaries in the world. Yet today, we see our religious liberties ebb and our social freedoms fail. This nation has stood for peace; yet in striving for peace apart from God, we find increasing unrest, worldwide wars, and ethnic conflict throughout the world.

The rapid rise in divorce removes many fathers from homes across the nation. As a result, at a national level, our children act like orphans. They are lost, insecure, in search of surrogate parents, willing to follow false leaders, and basically lawless. *Logically following the steps of the generation before it, this new generation does not just ignore God, but shakes its fist at Him.*

We, the Church

I once taught a summer Bible study for affluent men and their sons who were home from college on break. After ministering for a few weeks on the concerns of the young, one father spoke up and asked, "When are you going to teach something that relates to us and our sons?"

The Church can be like this man and choose to remain unaware of the impact our philosophies, practices, and policies have on our nation's youth. If we do, it will cost us a generation, and maybe even our own families. You see, what one generation accepts as a philosophy is taught to the next as truth. *If the Church chooses to not share Truth when we alone have the Truth, we doom our ability to influence society for years to come.*

Complacency is killing Christians. The attitude of *it won't happen to me and mine* doesn't work. In the homes of those who bury their heads in the sand, a killer stalks to steal ideals, values, and morals, and eventually it destroys the family.

Teenage violence strikes randomly. Anyone who chooses to remain unaware of the problem becomes part of the problem—and perhaps even the victim.

Ahaziah's Example

The wicked King Ahab and Queen Jezebel of Israel lived a life similar to what we live today. Jezebel was wholly aligned with the world. With a superior attitude, she cowed Ahab into subservience. When the offspring of their marriage, Ahaziah, took over their thrones, he arrogantly defied God and anything that stood for righteousness.

Children who lack proper discipline are boastful, arrogant, and proud. In the tango that the Church has danced with the world, we have allowed MTV and Hollywood to shape our children's ideas. Both of those groups blatantly shake their fists at anything righteous or godly. So what options are our offspring offered? They are given no direction.

Today the biggest thrills a young person can find are generally in the world, not in the Church. Our image of God is so weak that the Church often looks into the world and imitates what it sees there instead of imitating Christ. Many in churches today have not been willing to stand up for God at the expense of jobs, friends, and reputation. Most habitually and unthinkingly emulate the things of humankind and then wonder why their children drop out of church.

Elijah was not complacent. He did not dance the tango with the world, waltz with sin, or gaze fondly into the eyes of the wicked. When Ahaziah sent men to call him down from the mountain, Elijah instead called down fire to consume them. Only when the men came in humility, surrendering to Elijah and asking for their lives, did Elijah go with them.

> *Again, he sent a third captain of fifty with his fifty men. And the third captain of fifty went up, and came and fell on his knees before Elijah, and pleaded with him, and said to him: "Man of God, please let my life and the life of these fifty servants of yours be precious in your sight...."* *And the angel of the Lord said to Elijah, "Go down with him; do not be afraid of him." So he arose and went down with him to the king* (2 Kings 1:13-15).

When individuals within the Church wholeheartedly surrender to God, they will victoriously demand surrender from the world. That kind of Christianity is what we must offer the no-direction generation so that they might be convinced to turn from their wickedness and be able to survive their world.

CHAPTER 2

Where's the Beef?

For son dishonors father, daughter rises against her mother,
daughter-in-law against her mother-in-law; a man's
enemies are the men of his own household (Micah 7:6).

I remember watching a commercial for a fast-food restaurant chain that showed a little elderly woman traveling from one hamburger place to another. As each place presented her with a hamburger, she exclaimed, "Where's the beef?" Finally she came to the restaurant that offered a hamburger with some "beef," or substance. Her question became a rallying cry in that year's presidential election campaign. Amid all the hype and promises, voters wanted to know, "Where's the beef?"

In our fast-paced, fast-food society, a whole generation of people cries out, "Where's the beef? Where's the substance?" In effect they cry, "Where's the meaning, the value in life? What's my purpose?"

The fatherless generation is without purpose or direction: a no-direction generation.

In their search for identity, purpose, and meaning for their lives, many people seem crippled by an underlying sense of insecurities that in turn create despair and hopelessness. Because many in this no-direction generation are unfulfilled in their search, suicide rates—especially among young people—escalate. One psychiatrist pointed out, "Teens who commit suicide are not endeavoring to kill themselves, but to kill the hopelessness that is part and parcel of their daily existence."

According to the National Research Council, an estimated 7 million young Americans are at risk of failing to lead productive adult lives. This amounts to almost one-fourth of all 10- to 17-year-olds in America. "We believe that the problems of America's young people are getting significantly worse, not better. This is a human tragedy, and it is a national tragedy that will have a serious impact on us all."[1] What can be done to help them overcome this hopelessness?

Reversing the Trend

The secular community along with us the Church, realizes that this generation is in crisis. This is an important realization, insofar as it goes. But what can we do in the face of such a monumental crisis of identity? Some would throw up their hands and give up, but I do not believe we have to lose this generation. In their desperate need to find purpose, meaning, and identity, I believe this generation is ripe for the greatest outpouring of God's love and purpose we have ever seen.

So far this no-direction generation has tried to fill this need through sex, drugs, alcohol, music, gang activity, interpersonal relationships, and even lucrative careers. Their predecessors—

the *me generation*, the hippies, the beatniks, and all the others—tried somewhat the same thing. The philosophy of the 1960s and the 1970s—"do whatever feels good"—is one with a hollow ring. Their free living did not bring the promised liberation they hoped for; instead, many had to deal with previously unknown sexually transmitted diseases, soaring divorce rates, violence, and crime. The baby boomers' answer of sexual revolution did not produce fulfillment or genuine gratification. On the contrary, it produced today's generation of confused, aimless, and misdirected youth who also grasp for substance and meaning for their lives.

The negative trends in life of the 1970s and 1980s have escalated. In the 1990s we learned from a surprisingly eye-opening national survey:

- Almost one-third of all married Americans have had an extramarital affair.

- One out of five women states that she experienced date rape.

- One-fifth of American children say they lost their virginity by age 13.

- Six out of ten Americans have been victims of major crimes.

- One out of seven people carries a gun in his or her car.

- Seventy-two percent of the population do not know their next-door neighbor.

- Nine out of ten citizens lie regularly.

The same survey had this to say: "Americans are making up their own moral codes as they ease toward a century that threatens to be the wild, wild west all over again."[2] With this to contend with, is it any wonder that this generation feels hopeless? They are faced with bearing the consequences of the sins of the previous generation.

The moral decay of this nation will continue to escalate unless we, as the Church of Jesus Christ, become the examples of truth that will make these people free (see John 8:32).

Godly Role Models

Where are the heroes of our present generation? All too often, athletes, entertainers, politicians, and others have succumbed to the spirit of the age so aptly described by the apostle Paul:

> *But know this, that in the last days perilous times will come: for men will be lovers of themselves, lovers of money, boasters, proud, blasphemers, disobedient to parents, unthankful, unholy, unloving, unforgiving, slanderers, without self-control, brutal, despisers of good, traitors, head-strong, haughty, lovers of pleasure rather than lovers of God* (2 Timothy 3:1-4).

Godly role models, who will love and help this generation in their search for identity and direction, are greatly needed. People are looking for something with substance, with *beef*, to satisfy the longing of their souls. Not finding it, they turn to various substitutes in our counterfeit society that neither satisfy nor last. That is why many young people find substitute families in friends, peers, and even gangs.

Society's inconsistency between what authority figures say and do is readily perceived by today's generation. Because godly role models are lacking, youth are turning to other sources for guidance and direction. Thus many become rebellious toward any authority, even the authority they see in the Church.

David Wilkerson wrote in his May 1993 newsletter:

> Teenagers have lost all respect for authority—they are becoming hardhearted, sensual and violent. A 16-year-old lad from our church was shot and killed by his 15-year-old best friend—over a new coat and a pair of sneakers! The 15-year-old killed him and then stole the coat and shoes from the corpse. Worst of all, the teenage killer had no feelings of remorse. Education has failed our youth. Government has failed to reach them. Dead religion has turned them off! Eighty percent of all babies born to the young here in New York City are illegitimate. Sexual standards are nonexistent in city schools. There is only one hope left for the youth of our disintegrating American society: somehow God must reveal Himself to this lost generation.

The ministry I'm involved with here in Houston, Texas, faces the same scenario that David Wilkerson describes. The no-direction generation is a broken generation. Every day we talk to young people on the streets who face the consequences of a life without direction—pimps, prostitutes, crack dealers, homosexuals, those infected with AIDS, homeless wanderers. Each one is a broken person. It is only the love of Jesus that enables us to look beyond the person's lifestyle to see his or her broken heart.

This generation needs to see the reality of Jesus Christ manifested in the lives of people of integrity. They will look up to godly models who show God's love to them. Unfortunately, many of them have been abused in every possible way—exploited and used by older people who did not care about them. So, oblivious to the consequences of their lifestyle choices, they do not know how to accept responsibility for their actions. Death has no meaning for them. Though they hear that they are at high risk, the realization doesn't sink in until it is too late.

Giving Hope to the Hopeless

How do we help the no-direction generation? What is the missing link? All they did was follow in the footsteps of the previous generation's rebellion and rejection of God.

By rejecting God, they lost understanding of His love, purpose, and hope for their lives. A mediocre, lukewarm religion did not help either. The missing ingredient is a genuine passion for God that allows no room for mediocrity.

Mediocrity in the Church has birthed complacency in many Christians. That complacency has hindered us from effectively communicating God's purpose and direction to this generation.

We need to rise above our indifference and reach out to the no-direction generation with the power of the Holy Spirit and the grace of Jesus Christ. It is up to us, the Church, to give the hope and purpose that people need to find—a genuine identity and relationship with God through Jesus. In effect, *we need to become this generation's spiritual parents.*

These young people lost their vision of hope, and when that happened, they lost their purpose. Proverbs 13:12a says, "Hope deferred makes the heart sick." They have become a sick generation, a lawless generation. Without hope, they turn to drugs, alcohol, crime—and ultimately to anarchy and lawlessness. Gang violence and destruction are all cover-ups for their own emptiness and lack of hope. All sense of restraint and concern for others is gone because they themselves have no sense of hope. At that point, suicide becomes the answer.

Although Proverbs 13:12 says "hope deferred makes the heart sick," the second half of the verse also gives the remedy: "but when the desire comes, it is a tree of life" (Prov. 13:12b). Our responsibility is to bear the fruit of that tree and share it with them. As they begin to perceive the person of Jesus Christ within us, their hope will be restored. The only answer for this generation is to set hope before them—the hope that is in Jesus Christ. He is the hope and light of the world.

Why have the young people of today's society not been able to find the hope and light of the world? More than 60 percent of the teens I talk to tell me they have had "church experiences." Why couldn't they find Love Himself in the Church? They have heard about Jesus; they have seen the so-called Hollywood Jesus; they've experienced the institutionalized and religious Jesus; but they have not seen His reality demonstrated to them. They still cry out, "Give me something to believe in!" Like the little old woman in the commercial, they still cry, "Where's the beef?" They search for substance. They are tired of cheap and shallow platitudes.

The Challenge to the Church

May we as the Church give these young people the substance they search for. We can reach the fatherless generation with God's love. *This is the burning call to destiny that emanates from the heart of our heavenly Father—the call to a service of love.*

A fresh anointing is falling on the Church today—an anointing to be spiritual parents to this no-direction generation. We are called to *adopt* these orphans into the family of God. Let's reach out to the present generation with the love of Jesus, who will meet all their needs. It is time to stop talking about a godly life and to actually live it.

Edwin Louis Cole was so right when he stated, "The character of the Kingdom emanates from the character of the King." The King is looking for a people who will emulate His character— fathers and mothers in the Kingdom of God who are stamped with the seal of His Spirit. These people of character will be the *beef* this generation seeks. Only then will the longing in their souls begin to be satisfied.

Endnotes

1.   National Research Council, "Adolescents in High-Risk Settings," *Losing Generations* (Washington, DC: National Academy Press, 1993), 288.

2.   James Patterson and Peter Kim, "The Day America Told the Truth," *The Houston Chronicle*, April 29, 1991.

CHAPTER 3

A Father's Love

Fatherhood in America is being crushed in the colli-
sion between private needs and public pressures....
The message dads get is that they are not up to the
job. And a record number don't stick around—even
as fathers are needed more than ever.

—TIME MAGAZINE, June 28, 1993

What Is a Father?

Edwin Louis Cole, former President of the Christian Men's
Network, supplied a good definition for *father* in his book *Maximized Manhood.* He stated that a father is the one who guides,
guards, and governs in the home. He is the one who brings
proper disciplines, strengths, and direction to the family unit.
This is the biblical definition of fatherhood.

A father's heart is filled with love for his family. This love is
not a weak, insipid kind of sentimental love; it is a powerful,
giving love that always seeks the best interests of the child. A

father's love teaches through example as well as by precept. Andrew Murray points out that a successful parent "[studies] the art of speaking in the spirit of love....by striving to make his whole life an attractive example of what he has taught...."[1]

Unfortunately, the article in the June 28, 1993, issue of *Time* also said this:

> ...more children will go to sleep tonight in a fatherless home than ever in the nation's history. Talk to the experts in crime, drug abuse, depression, school failure, and they can all point to some study somewhere blaming those problems on the disappearance of fathers from the American family.[2]

The Dysfunctional Family

The word *dysfunctional* literally means "not working." Although it is overused and frequently misunderstood, it is an accurate description of families today. Most families simply are not working.

The baby boomers have grown up. Many have married, established their own families and careers, and are now ready to retire. They produced a generation that many called "the baby busters" (which implied that the financial boom of the 1980s would turn into a financial bust).

That was the American dream, right? Grow up, marry, and have kids. However, many baby boomers of the 1960s became members of the *me generation*. They became more focused on their own needs rather than on the needs of others. Many times their wants also became their *needs*. The marriages of many baby boomers consisted of two people living together who were willing to receive 100 percent in exchange for giving little or nothing. Spouses in such unions became leeches joined together in a feeding frenzy designed to suck the life from each other.

The idea of meeting one another's needs was translated by the me generation into this: "You must meet my needs." Consequently, commitment was passé and the sentence, "Divorce is granted," has echoed throughout the courts all over the country.

As a result, between 50 and 60 percent of young people in America grow up in single-parent homes. Even in many homes where both mother and father are present, children grow up with absentee parents—parents more focused on establishing their careers than their families. Intimacy and commitment—key ingredients of true love—seem to be missing altogether.

A secular model has uprooted the biblical concept of family—one that required both a father and mother. When children do not have proper bonding and intimacy with both parents, a breach or a form of spiritual schizophrenia envelops a child. This emotional tearing in a neglected child causes problems of identity, low self-esteem, and depression. Public schools are now faced with millions of these kids. Just look at the results of the breakdown of the American home:[3]

- Children from broken families are nearly twice as likely as those in two-parent families to drop out of high school.
- More than one-third [of the children] experienced moderate or severe depression even five years after their parents divorced.
- Seventy percent of all juveniles in state reform institutions come from fatherless homes.

Is it any wonder, then, that this present generation cannot understand the love of a heavenly Father? In many ways, we have brought the evils of society upon ourselves. So many have never known any kind of intimacy with their earthly fathers, even when they live in the same house. Some have been abused by their earthly fathers—sexually, emotionally, and physically.

In too many homes across our land, even fathers who are present have failed to become the leaders they were called to be. Having grown up without proper male role models themselves, many of them did not have any idea of what fatherhood really entails.

Ultimately people need to find a relationship with God the Father. He is the only One who can give them purpose and meaning to their lives. This fatherless, orphaned generation needs those who will show them the love of their heavenly Father. Without proper, godly role models in the home, young people are left to find their own way through the journey of life.

Searching for My Father

Several years ago, I had the opportunity to share my testimony with Sheila Walsh on the Christian Broadcasting Network's 700 Club. I told how, when I was growing up, I wanted to succeed in everything I could. All my life I strived for success and acceptance. I tried to find identity through academics and athletics, but they did not fulfill my deepest needs. When those things failed, I looked for acceptance and intimacy through friends and what I thought was love. It was all to no avail. Eventually, I followed a dark path of loneliness littered with the garbage of drugs, alcohol, and lawlessness.

I told Sheila that I thought the missing link in my life was my real father. I never really knew him. I had not seen him since I was about 9 years old; I was 21 when I began searching for him. Even though my mother and stepfather loved me, I somehow felt that I would never truly be a complete person until I found my father once more. Then, I thought, the cloud of confusion and emotional turmoil would lift from my life.

In Houston, Texas, I found and met my father. It was good to put some of the puzzle pieces of my life back together, but still I had not filled the longing in my soul.

Sheila Walsh responded with an awesome observation. I believe it was inspired by the Holy Spirit, both for me and for the fatherless generation around us. "It is interesting that Doug said he thought the search was for his father. And in a real sense it was, because each of us has a heavenly Father who cares for us very much. Doug was really searching for his heavenly Father." That was so true. My search for identity and the longing in my soul was not complete until I finally surrendered to the Lord.

Like the prodigal son, I had to return to my true Father in order to regain purpose, meaning, and identity. This is the deepest need of today's generation as well. The fatherless generation needs to know the truth about their heavenly Father's love for them.

For God so loved the world that He gave His only begotten Son, that whoever believes in Him should not perish but have everlasting life (John 3:16).

Returning to the Father

Fathers and sons, mothers and daughters—all of us—need to

see how our opulent, free-living, and profligate lifestyles are harming us and our society. Like the prodigal son in the Gospel of Luke, we have wasted our substance with riotous living. Soon there will be nothing left.

> *But when he had spent all, there arose a severe famine in that land, and he began to be in want. …And he would gladly have filled his stomach with the pods that the swine ate, and no one gave him anything* (Luke 15:14,16).

Eventually the prodigal son "came to himself" (Luke 15:17). He came to his senses, and he remembered where his safe place, his security, and his happiness could be found. He returned to his father. When he did so, he repented of his self-centered lifestyle.

> *"…Father, I have sinned against heaven and in your sight, and am no longer worthy to be called your son." But the father said to his servants, "Bring out the best robe and put it on him, and put a ring on his hand and sandals on his feet. …for this my son was dead and is alive again; he was lost and is found." And they began to be merry* (Luke 15:21-24).

I was that prodigal son. I thought I would find my answers from my earthly father. But it was only when I returned to my heavenly Father that I could receive God's promise for my life:

> *"…Son, you are always with me, and all that I have is yours"* (Luke 15:31).

What a glorious reunion! What an awesome revelation! This

is the message our fatherless generation needs to hear: *Return to your Father.*

A Fatherless Nation

Just as children without a father's teaching and discipline follow a path of rebellion and lawlessness, so does a nation whose people neglect their responsibilities to be what God has ordained. This generation has no understanding of the father in the home, much less of the Father in Heaven. Thus, without the direction and discipline of our heavenly Father in society, we will continue to see a rise in violence, immorality, and lawlessness in our communities. These are realities we must face. They are the inevitable consequences of fatherlessness.

Human effort and wisdom only go so far. Giving condoms in schools, providing psychologists in prisons, and implementing other man-made measures in an effort to stem the tide of lawlessness will not work. Gun-control laws and drug enforcement methods are attempts to help control crimes of violence, but even so, nearly every school in our society (including some parochial schools) has had to deal with students bringing guns. Daily, school officials face the issues surrounding drugs, sexually transmitted disease, teenage pregnancies, and violence.

It seems that the more we try to prevent these problems, the worse they become. We even see this on a worldwide scale. Efforts to bring about world peace through the United Nations and other organizations do not appear to be working. Great unrest and ethnic discord still exist in spite of international efforts to ease these tensions. Why? We're trying to bring about peace through man-made efforts instead of going to the Prince of Peace who said, "Follow Me" (Mark 10:21). There can be no peace without the Prince of Peace. Similarly, any society that rebels against the heavenly Father will always become lawless and rebellious. Righteousness, peace, and love can never be legislated; they come in only one way—through an intimate and personal relationship with the Lord Jesus Christ. There is only one way to the Father, and that is through the Son.

> *Jesus said to him, "I am the way, the truth, and the life. No one comes to the Father except through Me"* (John 14:6).

The Generation That Forgot God

Not only have we rejected our heavenly Father, but we have also forsaken the founding fathers of our nation. Society has asked for a bill of divorcement from the Church of Jesus Christ—the Church upon which the founding fathers based our society. Instead of seeking the freedom *of* religion that the U.S. Constitution guarantees, many are seeking freedom *from* religion.

We demand our own way. In effect, we defy God by shaking our fists in His face. Educators, politicians, lawmakers, and other leaders have turned away from our godly heritage. When they did, they severed the tree from its roots. Such a tree will eventually die without the moisture and nutrients it so desperately needs. This is the scenario in America today. God's standards of righteousness have been forgotten, with new "standards" being raised in their place. People pick and choose what is right and wrong *for them,* often according to their feelings.

A gradual desensitization permits us, including some Christians, to accept things once profane and obscene as now okay and even commonplace. Many have virtually no respect for any authority, even God's authority. Those who do take a stand for righteousness are openly and relentlessly mocked. It seems as if America is shouting, "We don't want God!"

In actuality, people do want God and His blessings. Most simply want them on *their* terms, not *His*. God becomes whomever or whatever they want to conceive Him to be. Forgetting that God created them in His own image, they try to recreate God in their own image. The result is disaster.

Time magazine subtitled an article in this way: "The Baby Boom Goes Back to Church, and Church Will Never Be the Same."[4] Cafeteria-style, people choose churches that seem palatable to them. Within the church, they choose what they want to believe. When uncomfortable, they leave to pick another church or to find God in a New Age context.

The nation that long led the evangelical movement, that became the hub of world missions, that set the pace and led in spiritual priorities, has lost its vision, its purpose, its direction, and its focus. *Once a nation with a strong heavenly Father, we have become a fatherless nation—a nation that has forgotten God.* Now we set the pace in the opposite direction. Other nations look to us, not for spiritual direction, but for the latest fads in music, entertainment, fashion, and technology.

Small wonder, then, that homosexuality is being taught to public school students as an "alternative lifestyle." Abortion is legal. Pornography is a "therapy" recommended by some psychologists and counselors. Television tells us that adultery and fornication are normal and portrays violence as an acceptable way of dealing with anger. Victims are punished; perpetrators are set free.

God ordained America to be a nation that would honor Him, but we have turned our backs on Him. We have gone after a multitude of other gods. Though He wants to be "a father of the fatherless, a defender of widows" (Ps. 68:5a), He cannot fulfill that desire of His heart unless we turn back to Him.

God has a special place in His heart for those who are poor, destitute, lost, and forgotten. He loves the fatherless orphans of our land, and He truly wants to pour out His Spirit upon this generation. He wants to become the Father that this generation has never known. He wants to wrap His arms around His widowed and divorced Church and love it back to wholeness and vitality. He wants to prepare the Bride (the Church of Jesus Christ) for the return of His Son.

The Father's call to this fatherless generation is to fulfill its destiny. He's looking for a people and a nation whom He can entrust with His mission and His purpose. Such a people will find their fulfillment, identity, and purpose in Him.

> *Blessed is the nation whose God is the Lord* (Psalm 33:12a).

Endnotes

1.   Andrew Murray, *The Children for Christ: Thoughts for Christian Parents on the Consecration of the Home Life* (New York: A.D.F. Randolph & Co., 1887), 120.

2.   Nancy R. Gibbs and Ann Blackman "Where Are All the Fathers?" *Time Magazine*, June 16, 2007.

3.   Ibid.

4.   Richard N. Ostling and Jordan Bonfante, "The Church Search," *Time Magazine*, April 5, 1993.

CHAPTER 4

A Nation of Orphans

It is the duty of all nations, as well as of men, to own their dependence upon the overruling power of God and to recognize the sublime truth announced in the Holy Scriptures and proven by all history, that those nations only are blessed whose God is the Lord.

—ABRAHAM LINCOLN

The Founding Fathers

The foundation of the United States of America was firmly laid upon the rock-solid teachings of God's Word. The founding fathers venerated the Scriptures and literally laid down their lives so future generations of Americans could enjoy the scriptural freedoms these men so dearly prized. The nation they founded, the nation they gave their lives for, was to be a nation under God. They knew that God would bless America if her citizens would serve the one true God. In the atmosphere of God's love and teachings, they knew that Americans from all backgrounds would be able to find their hope, purpose, freedom, and identity.

Look, for example, at what Christopher Columbus wrote in his journal:

> It was the Lord who put it in me to sail from here to the Indies. The fact that the Gospel must be preached to so many lands—that is what convinced me. Charting the seas is but a necessary requisite for the fulfillment of the Great Commission of our glorious Saviour.[1]

This same Christ-centered, God-glorifying attitude gave all the founding fathers a sense of divine purpose and mission in establishing the United States of America. These men were not deists, as so many historians have suggested; instead they were Christians who believed in the power of prayer and God's Word. George Washington wrote,

> Thou gave Thy Son to die for me; and hast given me assurance of salvation, upon my repentance and sincerely endeavoring to conform my life to His holy precepts and example.

Only a blood-washed, born-again believer could make such a statement. Washington added the phrase, "So help me God," to the presidential inauguration oath. He stated, "Do not let anyone claim to be a true American if they ever attempt to remove religion from politics."

Twentieth-century historians and educators have erased such

material from public school textbooks, but it behooves every American to realize that the roots of our nation go deeply into a rich soil of Christian grace, mercy, and love.

It is said that Thomas Jefferson was the most irreligious of early American presidents. Even if that is the case, notice what he had to say about God:

> God who gave us life gave us liberty. Can the liberties of a nation be secure when we have removed a conviction that these liberties are a gift of God? Indeed I tremble for my country when I reflect that God is just, and that His justice cannot sleep forever.

Jefferson's concern is entirely scriptural, and it needs to be our concern today. Orphaned America has forgotten its roots. We have failed to understand that the liberties we enjoy (but are now being seriously challenged) were God's gift to us. So many have forgotten that God's nature is just, that He will reward us according to our faith and righteousness, that He expects us to follow the precepts of His Word. As Jefferson prophesied, His justice will not sleep forever.

Moral Bankruptcy

The founding fathers responded wholeheartedly to God's burning call of destiny—to found America on His precepts. The purpose and destiny of America was clear to these godly leaders. They knew the Word of God. In fact, the Bible was their primary source of guidance in all matters related to government, lawmaking, and day-to-day living. They believed and treasured the psalmist's words:

> *Your word is a lamp to my feet and a light to my path. I have sworn and confirmed that I will keep Your righteous judgments* (Psalm 119: 105-106).

America's blessings are due to its founding fathers. They willingly went against the odds, faced innumerable hardships, and sacrificed everything they had to adhere to their vision. Many lost homes and possessions for the sake of something far beyond sheer human wisdom and logic. They paid the price—many even gave the ultimate sacrifice of life itself, as did the first Christians—that we might benefit. In this present hour of national crisis, God is calling others who will take up this same mantle to become spiritual founding fathers (and mothers) to reach this orphaned generation with the good news that their Father in Heaven invites them to find true freedom and abundant life in Him.

By rejecting the godly foundations and principles on which America was established, by denying our roots and our founding fathers, we have made the United States of America a fatherless nation. We have willfully walked out from under the umbrella of God's protective care. The result is seen on every street corner, in the schools and churches, in the media, on the stage, in the newspapers, and in government halls. It is moral bankruptcy. We have lost the vision that was bequeathed to us, and we have lost the blessing. Now we are gradually losing our freedoms as well.

Where there is no revelation, the people cast off restraint; but happy is he who keeps the law (Proverbs 29:18).

Like the prodigal son, America has taken the inheritance that the sacrificial investments of our founding fathers paid for and trashed it on the garbage dump of personal pleasure and self-aggrandizement. The handwriting is on the wall, and unless we face it, deal with it, and take proactive steps to change it, this moral bankruptcy will collapse America just as it did the earlier empires of Greece, Rome, Babylon, and the Soviet Union.

America has received what it asked for, and regrettably so has the Church. The curtain of judgment is falling. Yet as it falls, God still desires to pour out His mercy upon this orphaned generation. He longs for the people of this nation, and those around the world, to seek Him.

Even though America has given the Church a "letter of divorcement," it is truth that will prove to be America's best friend. As the Church proclaims prophetic truth to our leaders and people, God will move in our midst.

But the hour is coming, and now is, when the true worshipers will worship the Father in spirit and truth; for the Father is seeking such to worship Him. God is Spirit, and those who worship Him must worship in spirit and truth (John 4:23-24).

From every perspective, it seems illogical for a nation or an individual to turn a cold shoulder to a loving Father who wants to bless His children. *God deeply desires to be the Father who guides, guards, and governs this nation.* He wants to take care of us. In the midst of the shaking and trials coming upon this world, the question is, Will we allow Him to do His work in us so He can do His work through us? Will we seek to fulfill His will and not our own? Will we take the responsibility to become spiritual parents to an orphaned generation and nation?

We need to have the very life of God flow through us. We need for the Father to endue us with power from on high so we will truly be temples of the Holy Spirit wherever we go. God is challenging us to be a people whose heart-cry is, "Father, Your will, not mine, be done" (see Luke 22:42). Let us determine to persevere and lift high above our heads—for all the world to see— a standard of integrity and righteousness, a banner of His love.

A Clearer Focus

In November of 1988, I had the privilege of attending a prayer breakfast at which President George Bush was a guest speaker. As a proclamation for his term as President, he read Psalm 67. The President of the United States put forth a prophetic word for our nation when he read:

> *God be merciful unto us, and bless us; and cause His face to shine upon us....That Thy way may be known upon earth, Thy saving health among all nations. Let the people praise Thee, O God; let all the people praise Thee. O let the nations be glad and sing for joy: for Thou shalt judge the people righteously, and govern the nations upon earth....Let the people praise Thee, O God; let all*

the people praise Thee. Then shall the earth yield
her increase; and God, even our own God, shall
bless us. God shall bless us; and all the ends of the
earth shall fear Him (Psalm 67 KJV).

God desires to gain the attention of what was once a great Christian nation. He wants us to turn our focus back on Him. I believe the Lord was speaking prophetically to America through the passage President Bush read. Even in His righteous judgment and authority over the nations, there is mercy and blessing. Perhaps without realizing it, President Bush was prophetically asking God to bring merciful judgment to America. In order for God to be able to bless us and to be known among the ends of the earth—that we may respectfully honor and fear Him—He must have our attention. Sometimes He gets it through natural disasters (which are occurring with more frequency and intensity than ever before) and other calamities; at other times through personal crises.

We need to get a clearer focus of who God is, what His plan for the nation is, and who we are as His creatures. During a television interview, I was asked if I thought God would judge the United States or bring revival—as if the two possibilities are mutually exclusive. My answer to the interviewer was, "God will bring both." His mercy ever continues, even in the midst of judgment. We must never forget that God is not willing for anyone to perish; He wants all to come to repentance (see 2 Pet. 3:9). We know this is true because He sent His Son to pay the high price of brutally dying on the cross at Calvary. He judged us with a righteous judgment through His Son, Jesus Christ. The work of Christ on the cross justified us in the sight of God. This is His choice for us. However, we are the ones who choose judgment for ourselves when we do not seek His wisdom and guidance. We must ever remember that when we do not feel near to God, we're the ones who moved away—not Him.

Merciful Judgment

It is the mercy of God in the midst of His judgment that leads us to pull down all our false gods and look solely upon Him. His goodness leads us to repentance, but sometimes it takes the hard things of life to get our attention, to make us truly sorry for our disobedience, and to motivate us to change by seeking His help. As someone said, "Trouble leads us to Jesus."

God wants to give us a life more abundant than we've ever experienced. He wants this nation of orphans to receive His goodness. Even in the midst of the greatest economic, political, and moral shakings of history, God's mercy can be found. He is the God who is here, and He wants to pour out His blessings upon us. Jesus said,

> *I have come that they may have life, and that they may have it more abundantly* (John 10:10b).

This is the message that the fatherless generation needs to see and hear. We are living in the time that was prophesied long ago, the time described in the Book of Hebrews:

> *. . . much more shall we not escape if we turn away from Him who speaks from heaven, whose voice then shook the earth; but now He has promised, saying, "Yet once more I shake not only*

the earth, but also heaven." ... [So] that the things which cannot be shaken may remain (Hebrews 12:25-27).

A tremendous shake-up is taking place in America and around the world. The only things that will be able to withstand this shaking process are the Word of God, the true Church of Jesus Christ, and individual believers who know their Father— the foundational blocks of America. What is the purpose of this shaking and quaking of heaven and earth? It is to draw the "spiritual orphans" of the world to Jesus Christ.

Church Quake

When God judges a nation or a people, He begins within the house of God. This shaking is beginning in the Church. The Father in Heaven permits His consuming fire to burn the dross out of our lives to refine our faith. A faith tested in this way becomes an enduring faith. The result of this purging is the refining of God's people, His Church, and society. As God's people are purified, society will be affected in positive ways. That happens because God's people are the salt of the earth— and the saltier the people of God become, the more thirsty people in the world will become for God. Then with their focus on Him, God can produce a relationship with anointing, power, and fruitfulness.

Yes, in the end times there is a great judgment and a great revival. The judgment has begun—the revival is right around the corner. We must persevere in prayer, godly living, and witnessing so the revival fires will flare in every city, village, and town.

When individuals turn their hearts away from God, they tend to compensate for the loss by saying, "I want it *my* way! I will control my own destiny." In First Samuel 8, the people of God began to cry, "We want to be like other people. Give us a king!" (See First Samuel 8:5.) They didn't seem to understand that God, the Father, was the greatest King of all. They were no longer satisfied with Him.

We in the United States of America have copied their poor example. We would rather serve any idol than God—money, fame, sexual pleasure, self-interest, etc. When we do this, we say to God, "You are not doing it our way. We want a king who is different from You." People believe that they gain newfound freedoms when they turn from God, but in actual fact they gain newfound bondages that seriously curtail individual freedom.

In First Samuel 8, we read that God told Samuel to let the people have what they wanted (see 1 Sam. 8:7). (He gives us what we ask for.) The results were disastrous, as they always are when we allow other things or people to take the place of God. The worst disaster for all the Israelites who wanted a king was foretold to them by Samuel:

> *And you will cry out in that day because of your king whom you have chosen for yourselves,* **and the Lord will not hear you in that day** (1 Samuel 8:18).

God has allowed us to have a king as the world has. We desperately need the King of kings and the Lord of lords to rule this nation once again. However, God cannot answer the prayers of a rebellious nation. He cannot hear our prayers, unless we repent. If we regard iniquity in our hearts, God cannot hear us. That is why we are suffering the consequences of our choices.

For many years, Jack Hayford has been a person who has spoken into my life personally, at times, and through his leadership as well. I met him first at a conference in Houston in the 1990s and was then invited to speak at Love L.A. In 1994, he had a prophetic word for us at a conference of the National Religious Broadcasters in Washington, D.C. He challenged the political and religious leaders who were present that God cares more about us as individuals than about our churches, ministries, and organizations. "God loves you enough," he said, "to let you lose it [our ministries] to keep you."[2] Shortly afterward, we began to see the fall of many prominent ministries. God's merciful judgment was at work, and He began with the house of God.

Everything that can be shaken will be shaken. The idols will come crashing down because God loves the idolaters. He wants them to seek Him as their source of strength. Jesus pointed out, "He who falls on this stone will be broken to pieces, but he on whom it falls will be crushed" (Matt. 21:44 NIV). Either we allow ourselves to be humbled before God so He can heal and lead us, or we continue to rebel against Him and eventually find ourselves under His righteous judgment. Therefore, we as a people, Church, and nation can make the choice to walk in righteousness and be blessed or to suffer the consequences of our rebellion. The fatherless generation will not be able to escape if they neglect so great a salvation. (See Hebrews 2:3.)

The words of the prophet Isaiah ring true today:

Say to the righteous that it shall be well with them, for they shall eat the fruit of their doings.

Woe to the wicked! It shall be ill with him, for the reward of his hands shall be given him. As for My people, children are their oppressors, and women rule over them. O My people! Those who lead you cause you to err, and destroy the way of your paths (Isaiah 3:10-12).

The prophet was speaking for God. First he declares that we will eat the fruit of our doings. Today the fruit of hardened hearts and selfish ambitions is the increase in gang activity, crime, and persecution. Then the prophet describes what happens when a generation loses respect for all authority. We have a generation rebellious toward all authority—and it is being led astray by our leaders. Conversely, if we give our hearts to the Lord, we will ever walk in the paths of righteousness for His name's sake. His glorious promise will follow: "Surely goodness and mercy shall follow me all the days of my life; and I will dwell in the house of the Lord forever" (Ps. 23:6).

Unwittingly, the orphaned generation of our present day has long been crying, "We'll do it our way. Give us a different king than You." God has graciously granted their request. Let us, before America follows the end of the nations in the Bible, lead our generation to the eternal Rock that is higher than anything mankind can offer or conceive. He came to heal the brokenhearted, set the captives free, and break the chains of bondage so that we could walk with Him in victory every day. It is only by turning to Him that we can prevent the rock of God's judgment from falling on us.

From the Constitution Hall in Philadelphia, the words of John Adams continue to warn us. I pray that his words will reverberate in every government hall, church, and home of our nation:

Our Constitution was made only for a moral and religious people. It is wholly inadequate for the government of any other.

Endnotes

1. Christopher Columbus Journal, 1492 voyage.

2. Jack Hayford (sermon, National Religious Broadcasters Conference, Washington, D.C., April 1994).

CHAPTER 5

The State of the Union

The highest glory of the American Revolution was this: it connected, in one indissoluble bond, the principles of civil government with the principles of Christianity.

— JOHN QUINCY ADAMS

In God We Trust

Every piece of currency issued in America proclaims "in God we trust." Our Pledge of Allegiance to the Flag points out that we are a nation "under God." But trusting in God requires much more than lip service; it is a life commitment to follow the Lord. This is the kind of commitment our founding fathers expected our nation to keep. They knew the truth of Proverbs 3:5-6:

> *Trust in the Lord with all thine heart; and lean not unto thine own understanding. In all thy ways acknowledge Him, and He shall direct thy paths* (Proverbs 3:5-6 KJV).

These principles of trust apply to individuals, churches, communities, and nations. God is waiting for our nation to return to these fundamental, foundational principles so the "indissoluble bond" that ties America to Christianity will never be severed.

National Trends

In the same way that families are drifting away from a father's authority, so is the ship of state drifting far from its original moorings. Many people regard God as a hobby rather than as the almighty God of the universe. A kind of divine Santa Claus image has replaced the concept of God as Father. The stance of the media has contributed to this switch. Garry Willis pointed out, "Media people are ignorant of religion, afraid of it and try to stay away from it."[1]

Stephen Carter, Professor of Law at Yale University, wrote *The Culture of Disbelief,* an informative book that discusses this national trend toward irreligion.[2] Carter points out that American liberalism tends to discount and mistrust people who take public stands that concern their religious convictions. The U.S. Catholic bishops agree with his observations. Their 1992 statement concludes that there is a "strong tendency to privatize faith, to push it to the margins of society."[3] The result? Some believers are ashamed to let people know they are Christians.

Because of these trends, it is becoming increasingly difficult for the Church of Jesus Christ to be taken seriously by intellectuals, the media, educational institutions, and society at large. The Church, therefore, often finds itself playing the defensive position rather than taking the offense by becoming the seasoning of society.

A Clash of Cultures

The Freedom Forum First Amendment Center at Vanderbilt University points out that a "wide chasm" and an "unhealthy distrust" exist between "two alien cultures... one rooted largely in a search for facts and the other grounded in a discovery of faith beyond fact." The culture of disbelief and the culture of belief are at odds with each other almost to the point of total polarization.

The findings from a survey of nearly one thousand clergy and journalists suggest that both secular forces and religious groups employ false stereotyping and misreading of motives.[4] These tactics lead to deep mistrust between the two *cultures*. Thus, a full-scale war is raging all around us.

Social scientist James Q. Wilson writes that "the powers exercised by the institutions of social control have been constrained, and people, especially young people, have embraced an ethos that values self-expression over self-control."[5] This war has escalated in the academic institutions of our land. One of its bloodiest battlegrounds is found in the minds of our fatherless young people.

In 1940, teachers reported the worst problems in our public schools as being these: talking out of turn; chewing gum; making noise; running in hallways; cutting in line; dress code infractions; and littering. In contrast, in 1990, teachers identified the following problems as being most significant: drug abuse; alcohol abuse; pregnancy; suicide; rape; robbery; and assault. Without the leadership of an earthly father who derives his authority from the heavenly Father, young people today find themselves adrift on a turbulent sea of doubt and confusion. Many have lost sight of the shoreline and have no compass to guide them.

It is time for believers to take the offensive. We must lead society back to God and the Bible. The apostle Paul showed us how to launch this offensive; he gave us advice that enables us to engage in cultural warfare effectively and victoriously. He wrote:

> *And do not participate in the unfruitful deeds of darkness, but instead even expose them* (Ephesians 5:11 NASB).

He then went on to explain how we are to fight the good fight of faith—by being dressed in the whole armor of God and by being "strong in the Lord and in the power of His might" (Eph. 6:10).

Paul also stressed the importance of prayer as a weapon to be used in our current cultural conflicts:

> *Praying always with all prayer and supplication in the Spirit, being watchful to this end with all perseverance and supplication for all the saints* (Ephesians 6:18).

We will win the battle if we stay focused on our calling, if we make sure we wear the full armor that God provides for us, and if we determine in our hearts to take the offensive by exposing the works of darkness. In so doing, we must ever be mindful of this truth:

> *For we do not wrestle against flesh and blood, but against principalities, against powers, against the rulers of the darkness of this age,*

against spiritual hosts of wickedness in the heav-enly places (Ephesians 6:12).

The conflict of cultures is truly a spiritual war that has left countless victims lying in the trenches, streets, homes, and insti-tutions of our land. These casualties of war will remain hopeless unless God's people take decisive action. The tragedy is that so many of these victims are the young people.

Clearly, we need a cultural renewal. That will not happen through legislation, though, because we know morality and spir-ituality cannot be legislated into existence. Rather, it requires that hearts be changed by the Spirit of God. As the Church of Jesus Christ, we can help usher in the revival that America needs. Through our commitment, our intercession, and our love, we will see the fulfillment of God's promise given through the prophet Joel:

And it shall come to pass afterward that I will pour out My Spirit on all flesh; your sons and your daughters shall prophesy, your old men shall dream dreams, your young men shall see visions. . . . And I will show wonders in the heavens and in the earth . . . (Joel 2:28,30).

What a glorious day that will be!

Does Crime Pay?

Lawlessness and violence thrive in our society. The number of imprisoned people is at an all-time high. By the end of

1991, 825,000 people were incarcerated in America's prisons. It costs society approximately $25,000 per year to maintain each of these prisoners. As of 2007, the United States Department of Justice reported that "2,293,157 prisoners were held in federal or state prisons or in local jails—an increase from year end 2006."[6]

The cause of such high crime rates is not socioeconomic; it is spiritual. As Aleksandr Solzhenitsyn pointed out, "The West... has been undergoing an erosion and obscuring of high moral and ethical ideals. The spiritual axis of life has grown dim."[7]

The cost of crime for the victims of our society is incalculable. Speaking in terms of cash, the aggregate cost of crime for victims back in 1984 was $92.5 billion. "In fiscal year 2006, federal, state, and local governments spent an estimated $214 billion for police protection, corrections, and judicial and legal activities, a 5.1 percent increase over the previous year."[8] This does not include the emotional toll that violence extracts from its victims.

The Wall Street Journal, in showing that the fastest growing segment of our nation's criminal population consists of children and young people, observed, "The tragedy of this system is that because he is so rarely made to pay for his crime, the juvenile offender doesn't get the message that crime doesn't pay. He may not even get the message that what he's done is reprehensible in any sense."[9] Many of these young criminals are truly fatherless, and most know nothing of a father's authority.

When we combine child crime, child poverty, child abuse, infant mortality, and other factors related to our children, we quickly recognize that the state of our union is weakening at a rapid pace.

When Will We Ever Learn?

Suicide in the '90s was the second greatest teenage killer in the United States, according to Dr. Bob Anstine and Dr. Richard Arno in their book *Counseling the Suicidal/Teen Suicide*.[10] Although this tragic trend is decreasing, suicides amongst teens are still at an alarming rate, accounting for 12 percent of the deaths amongst youth.[11] It is believed that for every successful suicide, there are approximately 100 unsuccessful attempts. Suicidal young people I've worked with indicate that a pervading sense of loneliness, hopelessness, and purposelessness drives them to attempt suicide.

A fatherless generation of orphans goes through the early years of life feeling rejected and devoid of meaning. Such orphans may turn to sex in an effort to find love. Often, such early sexual activity leads to teenage pregnancies. The number of unmarried teenagers getting pregnant nearly doubled over two decades— and now, one in every four pregnancies ends in abortion. Despite a continual decline, the teenage pregnancy rate in the United States still remains among the highest of any industrialized nation.[12]

The number of divorces in America increased nearly 200 percent in the three decades, leaving many of our children and young people feeling fatherless. Less than 60 percent of all children today live with their biological, married parents. As William Galston writes, "The economic consequences of a parent's absence are often accompanied by psychological consequences, which include higher than average levels of youth suicide, low intellectual and education performance, and higher than average rates of mental illness, violence and drug use."[13]

Secular society recognizes these problems, and educational and governmental institutions attempt to deal with them. Regrettably, we are losing the war on drugs, the war against AIDS, and all the other social battles we face today. Giving condoms to kids is like offering adhesive bandages to those who are mutilating themselves.

I once organized an evangelistic outreach at a university. In preparation for the outreach, I noticed in the student newspaper a large advertisement. It was an editorial about using "condom sense," inferring that people should use condoms.

This inspired me to write a tract called "The Condom Cover-Up." So often, our society wants us to cover up the problem instead of deal with its root issues. Similarly, abortion attempts to solve a problem that stems from intrinsic irresponsibility. Giving clean needles to drug addicts attempts to solve one problem by exacerbating another one. Sex education gives information, but it does not provide a clear-cut framework for building a person's character. Methadone therapy in the lives of heroin addicts simply substitutes one drug for another. "Just say no" sounds nice, but a slogan is useless in the life of a person who does not have a sound spiritual base on which to build. A fatherless person has a hard time saying "no."

Character building begins in the home. The biblical pattern is for the father to set the tone for values in the family. By his teaching and example, the father leads his children into understanding the difference between right and wrong. By putting God first in his life, a father teaches his family what godly values and virtues are. When the character of a man is transformed through Christ, his destiny as well as the direction of his home and family are determined. When the father refuses his God-given responsibility, the absence of direction leaves a void in the family. Remember, the family is the microcosm of the community, society, and nation.

Consider what Professor of Sociology David Poponoe of Rutgers University points out in "The Controversial Truth: Two-Parent Families Are Better":[14]

> In three decades of work as a social scientist, I know of few other bodies of data in which the weight of evidence is so decisively on one side of the issue: on the whole, for children, two-parent families are preferable...If our prevailing views on family structure hinged solely on scholarly evidence, the current debate would never have arisen in the first place.

This void did not exist for very long before being filled. Television has become the surrogate "father" in many American homes. Today the average American watches television a little more than 50 hours per week.[15] From this video "mentor," our children learn many things—especially inappropriate ways to resolve conflicts (often through blatant violence depicted on the screen), the degradation of human sexuality, and the *excitement* of an irreligious lifestyle. According to researchers, "...heavy exposure to televised violence is one of the causes of aggressive behavior, crime, and violence in society. Television affects youngsters of all ages, of both genders, at all socioeconomic levels and all levels of intelligence...It cannot be denied or explained away."[16] Sixty-seven percent of Americans believe the media has the greatest influence on children's values—more than church, parents, and teachers combined.[17]

The King of Kings

In the face of such discouraging statistics and the negative scenario painted by our society today, the true believer can still take heart. We know that our Lord is greater than "the prince of the power of the air" (Eph. 2:2).

> *You are of God, little children, and have overcome them, because He who is in you is greater than he who is in the world* (1 John 4:4).

Fathers who establish spiritual priorities in the home teach their children to "seek first the kingdom of God and His righteousness, and all these things shall be added to you" (Matt. 6:33). A family can rest in the sense of security provided by a godly father, and a nation can rest in the security of the heavenly Father who guards, guides, and governs in all its affairs.

> *Yet in all these things we are more than conquerors through Him who loved us* (Romans 8:37).

Endnotes

1.   Quoted in John Leo, "Boxing in Believers," *U.S. News and World Report,* September 12, 1993.

2.   Stephen Carter, *The Culture of Disbelief* (New York: Anchor Books, 1993).

3.   The C.J.S Catholic Bishops (1992).

4.   John Seigenthaler, "Bridging the Gap: Religion and the U.S. News Media, *The Freedom Forum First Amendment Center,* September 1994.

5. Quoted in William J. Bennett, "Quantifying America's Decline," *The Wall Street Journal,* March 15, 1993.

6. "Prison Statistics," *Bureau of Justice Statistics,* http://www .ojp.usdoj.gov/bjs/prisons.htm (accessed January 1, 2009).

7. Statement made during speech given by Russian Nobel Peace Prize author Aleksandr Solzhenitsyn.

8. "USDOJ Expenditure and Employment Statistics," *Bureau of Justice Statistics,* http://www.ojp.usdoj.gov/bjs/eande.htm (accessed January 1, 2009).

9. "The Young and the Violent," *The Wall Street Journal,* September 23, 1992, A16.

10. Dr. Bob Anstine and Dr. Richard Arno, *Counseling the Suicidal/Teen Suicide* (National Christian Counselors Association, 1991), 2.

11. CDC, National Center for Injury Prevention and Control, Office of Statistics and Programming, *Web-based Injury Statistics Query and Reporting System (WISQARS).* http://www .cdc.gov/ncipc/wisqars/ (accessed January 1, 2009).

12. National Center for Health Statistics, "Recent Trends in Teenage Pregnancy in the United States, 1990-2002," http://www .cdc.gov/nchs/products/pubs/pubd/hestats/teenpreg1990-2002/teenpreg1990-2002.htm (accessed January 2, 2009).

13. William Galston and Elaine Kamarck, "A Progressive Family Policy for the 1990s," *The Index of Leading Cultural Indicators*, ed. William J. Bennett, vol. 1 (Washington, D.C.: The Heritage Foundation/Empower America, 1993), 16.

14. D. Poponoe, "The Controversial Truth: Two-Parent Families Are Better," *The New York Times*, December 26, 1992.

15. Nielson Media Research, "Nielson Media Research Reports Television's Popularity Is Still Growing," http://www

.neilsonmedia.com/nc/portal/site/Public/menuitem (accessed January 2, 2009).

16.   L. D. Eron, "The Impact of Televised Violence," (testimony on behalf of the American Psychological Association before the Senate Committee on Governmental Affairs, Congressional Record, June 18, 1992).

17.   "Our Drug of Choice," *Christianity Today/Men of Integrity Magazine*, June 4, 2006.

CHAPTER 6

The State of the Church

I know your works, love, service, faith, and your patience; and as for your works, the last are more than the first. Nevertheless I have a few things against you, because you allow that woman Jezebel, who calls herself a prophetess, to teach and seduce My servants to commit sexual immorality and eat things sacrificed to idols (Revelation 2:19-20).

The Spirit of Jezebel

The Church today is doing great works. It is feeding the poor, holding youth services and outreaches to the community, and helping the sick. These works are all commendable, but there is one problem. The spirit of Jezebel has crept into the Church in America.

This Jezebel spirit is leading believers into committing spiritual adultery with her. Unknowingly, the Church is rejecting the fatherhood of God for a marriage to this adulterous spirit. Afraid to stand for righteousness, churches cower behind the mortal leaders of the land. In turn, these politicians and social activists regard the things of this world as more important than a covenant with God. Their covenant is with the kingdom of this world instead of with the Kingdom of God. Thus, they likewise prostitute themselves for the sake of personal gain. Such ungodly choices destroy the path of the righteous, cluttering it with obstacles and roadblocks.

God, in His mercy, gave Jezebel the chance to repent of her immorality.

> *And I gave her time to repent of her sexual immorality, and she did not repent. Indeed I will cast her into a sickbed, and those who commit adultery with her into great tribulation, unless they repent of their deeds* (Revelation 2:21-22).

Many of us would not have given Jezebel time to repent, but God did. How much more God has been longsuffering, persevering, patient, and merciful with the Church in this nation! If we do not heed His call, we will suffer for our own doings.

> *Or do you despise the riches of His goodness, forbearance, and longsuffering, not knowing that the goodness of God leads you to repentance?* (Romans 2:4)

It's Not My Fault—Is It?

Our apathy, complacency, and neglect have caused our

society's situation today. It's easy to point our fingers at the homosexuals, abortionists, adulterers, and other sinners with their sin-filled lifestyles, declaring that it's their fault. However, it's not what they are doing that is the problem—it is what *we* have *not* done.

God has given us time to repent, and we have not repented. Repentance does not mean asking for the Lord's forgiveness when we're under pressure. True repentance is realizing that change is in order—that it's absolutely necessary—even if it means we lose everything. You see, when we surrender our lives to the Lord, He takes away all that is not of Him in order to give us everything that is.

Dr. Edwin Cole stated, "You cannot compensate by sacrifice what you lose through disobedience."[1] We see many children today suffering negative consequences from choices made by their parents—children with AIDS, for example, or those with Fetal Alcohol Syndrome. "Crack babies" are hopelessly addicted to crack cocaine because of their mothers' choices. Often the parents will pray for help, yet not change their behavior. "God, have mercy. Won't You please intervene for the sake of my children, even though I have neglected my responsibilities? Could You please intervene in behalf of this nation, even though I have not done what I should?" God will answer only if we truly want to surrender to His Lordship.

In order for people to repent and return to the Father, we need to engage in intercessory prayer. God wants us to intercede for our children and our nation. He does not desire that anyone perish, but that everyone would come to repentance (see 2 Pet. 3:9). The ancient prophet Ezekiel revealed this merciful Father-heart of God:

So I sought for a man among them who would make a wall, and stand in the gap before Me on behalf of the land, that I should not destroy it; but I found no one (Ezekiel 22:30).

The Spirit of Revival in Judgment

God is patient; He is withholding His final judgment. The shaking the Church is now experiencing is to get the Church to judge itself.

For if we would judge ourselves, we would not be judged. But when we are judged, we are chastened by the Lord, that we may not be condemned with the world (1 Corinthians 11:31-32).

When God's people submit to this internal evaluation, voluntarily bowing to the chastisement of the Lord, God can pour out His spirit of revival. Judgment is in the midst of this revival, though; the two are not mutually exclusive. Within His judgment, however, mercy is still found. So it is much better for the people of God to receive judgment now, than to be judged throughout all eternity.

The Lord stands up to plead, and stands to judge the people. The Lord will enter into judgment with the elders of His people and His princes: "For you have eaten up the vineyard; the plunder of the poor is in your houses. What do you mean by crushing My people and grinding the faces of the poor?" says

*the Lord God of hosts. Moreover the Lord says:
"Because the daughters of Zion are haughty, and
walk with outstretched necks and wanton eyes,
walking and mincing as they go, making a jingling
with their feet"* (Isaiah 3:13-16).

The Church of Jesus Christ sometimes walks with a seductive spirit, in pride and arrogance. God says He will take away all of the Church's bracelets and jewelry, all the fine garments, purses, turbans, and robes. This applies to America as well. You see, He takes away these things because He will not allow any other gods before Him. He alone is the living God of this land. If it were not for the sake of the intercessors falling on their faces in brokenness before God in prayer, He would not even regard this nation.

*You shall not bow down to them nor serve them.
For I, the Lord your God, am a jealous God,
visiting the iniquity of the fathers upon the children to the third and fourth generations of those
who hate Me, but showing mercy to thousands, to
those who love Me and keep My commandments*
(Exodus 20:5-6).

Do you see how needy we have become? We suffer the results of our own doings and neglect (see Isa. 3). It is the righteous remnant of God's people who holds our nation and society together. The cycles of alcoholic families and welfare families are broken when someone stands in the gap both in prayer and in practical ways. Such spiritual fathers and mothers take steps to adopt this orphaned generation. In response to their prayers, His mercy will triumph over His judgment. He still desires to become the Father of this fatherless nation.

Drawing Near to God

During this time of shaking and judgment, some will plead for mercy. Others will raise their hands against God's anointed and all that is righteous. Still others believe that they will be OK. Because they happen to wear a "Christian" label, they believe they have *fire insurance.* God is not looking for a label; He is looking for a relationship.

God is looking for those who see beyond themselves—beyond their personal needs and wishes—and perceive the purpose of their lives for this generation. He desires to have a people who love Him for who He is. Such people will never dishonor Him, but will take a determined stand for righteousness.

> *Therefore, my beloved brethren, be steadfast, immovable, always abounding in the work of the Lord, knowing that your labor is not in vain in the Lord* (1 Corinthians 15:58).

Our Father in Heaven wants His children to enjoy His presence, to fellowship with Him forever. He wants us to know His voice and to walk in His ways. It is in an intimate place of relationship with the Lord that we will hear His voice and the direction He wants us to take. There we will draw near to hear what He has to say and so bring healing and hope to the lives of those in this generation.

Revival!

A revival will break loose among those who will listen to the voice of the Lord. Those who refuse spiritual unemployment, who get their hearts focused back on God, will see the greatest move of God that has ever occurred. Every false idol that exalted itself against the truth of God will come crashing down!

All this will come as we raise our voice in a stand for righteousness in the land. If we will heed the voice of the Lord and bow to Him, God will pour out a great anointing to proclaim the Gospel to the world. Let's turn our focus back to God so that we might reach this fatherless generation with the message of the Father's love.

My eyes were opened by the objective observations of a young minister from South Africa concerning our nation and the Church in America. Eugene came from Johannesburg to Houston to be part of our ministry for several months.

> My time in the States has been a tremendous one, especially traveling from one state to the other, seeing good sights and also experiencing all the blessings God has bestowed on this great nation. I do believe and know that the United States of America and the Church of America have been given a great responsibility to influence and make Jesus known to the nations of the world. In spite of all the materialism of the West and its prosperity, America has neglected her responsibility. Today, she exports more of her pornography and sin to the world than the world has ever seen.

"Righteousness exalts a nation, but sin is a reproach to any people" (Prov. 14:34). Changing the constitution, rewriting the history books, murdering babies, giving rights to immoral perverts, and getting rid of prayer in the public schools without giving priority to God and His Word is a direct result of a nation that is fallen. God's judgment has already begun in America. Praise be to God that there is a remnant that God is choosing that will stand for righteousness without compromise. Matthew 20:16 says that "many are called, but few chosen." What the Church needs to do in this time and age is to seek the face of God.

Eugene's observation is a word for the United States of America and the Christian people within her borders. It is a clear cry from the Father-heart of God. He wants His children to hear and take heed.

Shouldering the Responsibility

When the Church aborts its spiritual responsibilities, we have no right to point our fingers or blame those in the world. Although the world may act out its rebellion and divorce itself from God and the Church in the natural realm, it is actually following a pattern set by God's people. The world is simply reflecting what we have done in the spiritual realm through our neglect, apathy, and complacency.

Romans chapter 1 is a vivid description of God's judgment of ungodliness. Yet Romans chapter 2 warns those who think they escape judgment that they may be guilty of the very things for which they judge the world. The spiritual sins and negligence of the Church are eventually manifested in the world. Is this not a greater sin for those who know the truth? People in the world are simply following their natural instincts. We in the Church must not abort or divorce ourselves from our responsibilities; instead, we must accept the commission God has given us.

As the Church becomes more spiritually responsible, we will see a drastic change in the world around us. Instances of crime, illegitimacy, abortion, and all of the other evils of our present times will decline. Most importantly, the fatherless generation will no longer be Fatherless.

Endnote

1. Edwin Cole, *Maximized Manhood: A Guide to Family Survival*, (New Kensington, PA: Whitaker House, 2001).

CHAPTER 7

The State of the Family

Behold, I will send you Elijah the prophet before the coming of the great and dreadful day of the Lord. And he will turn the hearts of the fathers to the children, and the hearts of the children to their fathers, lest I come and strike the earth with a curse (Malachi 4:5-6).

Powerlessness

Looking at the state of the union and the state of the Church, we see that we have some serious issues to face and confront. These situations stem directly from the sense of fatherlessness that pervades our nation and our people.

Unfortunately, satan has launched an all-out offensive against fathers and families in our society. The frightening statistics tell the tale: half of our marriages end in divorce; millions of kids live in fatherless homes; more than one child in eight is raised on government welfare through Aid to Families With Dependent Children; 18 percent of children live in poverty; and so on.[1]

If matters weren't bad enough already, the American Enterprise Institute reports that teenage sexual activity will result in nearly one million pregnancies annually, leading to 406,000 abortions, 134,000 miscarriages, and 490,000 live births. Also, about three million teens will get sexually transmitted diseases within the year.[2]

In 1990, at least 1.6 million abortions were performed in the United States. Professor Mary Ann Glendon of Harvard's School of Law has stated that we have the most permissive abortion laws of any democracy in the world. Since abortion was legalized in 1973 by the Supreme Court's decision with *Roe v. Wade,* more than 49 million abortions have been performed in America.[3]

In 1990, nearly 3 million cases of child abuse were reported.[4] These cases involved all types of abuse: emotional, physical, sexual, and ritual. Government authorities attribute the rise in child abuse to substance abuse, stresses related to single parenthood, alcoholism, and financial pressures.

The number of divorces increased nearly 200 percent in three decades; the percentage of people getting married is at an all-time low. Young people, as well as older people, are living together without matrimony at alarming rates. Even older adults previously widowed or divorced are choosing to live together outside the bonds of marriage so they can keep their Social Security benefits.

Children of Divorce

Children are directly impacted by the divorce of their parents. Only 61 percent of all children in our nation today live in a traditional nuclear family with their married biological parents.[5] This rate is the lowest in the Western World.[6] Each year, over one million children suffer the divorce of their parents.[7] Millions of children in the United States now live in *blended families* with stepparents or siblings who are not blood relatives. Often these children are pulled between combative parents—living with each part-time and having to adjust to different rules in each household.

According to the U.S. Census Bureau, the number of traditional households declined sharply from 40 to 26 percent from 1970 to 1990.

One-parent families account for one-fourth of all the children in the United States. In the overwhelming majority of these homes, the mother is the single parent. Concerning these households, psychologist Urie Brondenbrenner of Cornell University writes in "Discovering What Families Can Do,"[8]

> Controlling for factors such as low income, children growing up in single-parent households are at a greater risk for experiencing a variety of behavioral and educational problems, including extremes of hyperactivity and withdrawal; lack of attentiveness in the classroom; difficulty in deferring gratification; impaired academic achievement; school misbehavior; absenteeism; dropping out; involvement in socially alienated peer groups; and the so-called 'teenage syndrome' of behaviors that tend to hang together—smoking, drinking, early and frequent sexual experience, and in the more extreme cases, drugs, suicide, vandalism, violence, and criminal acts.

In addition to these factors, SAT scores are declining while high school dropout rates are increasing. Though drug use is decreasing somewhat, teenage use of alcohol is on the rise. Our fatherless young people are behaving in ways that vividly reveal their need for a father's guidance, governing, and guarding. Their behaviors may even be a cry for a father. According to Curt Williams, the director of Youth Reach Houston (a home for troubled boys), in a survey of 603 boys in their program, only 16 had a healthy relationship with a father.

Father—the Priest in the Home

A priest's responsibility is to represent God to his parishioners and his parishioners to God. This is exactly a role of the father at home. It is also the role that this fatherless generation seeks someone to fill. God is looking for natural and spiritual fathers who will take the stance of Joshua:

> ... *choose for yourselves this day whom you will serve, whether the gods which your fathers served that were on the other side of the River, or the gods of the Amorites, in whose land you dwell. But as for me and my house, we will serve the Lord* (Joshua 24:15).

The apostle Paul gives us a beautiful picture of true Christian family living in the following steps:

1. *Submitting to one another in the fear of God* (Ephesians 5:21).

2. *Wives, submit to your own husbands, as to the Lord* (Ephesians 5:22).

3. *Husbands, love your wives, just as Christ also loved the church and gave Himself for her* (Ephesians 5:25).

4. *Children, obey your parents in the Lord, for this is right. "Honor your father and mother," which is the first commandment with promise: "that it may be well with you and you may live long on the earth"* (Ephesians 6:1-3).

5. *And you, fathers, do not provoke your children to wrath, but bring them up in the training and admonition of the Lord* (Ephesians 6:4).

Father—the Prophet in the Home

Prophets in the Old and New Testaments had two primary responsibilities: to speak forth God's Word to the people and to foretell the future (usually in matters related to divine justice and judgment). Prophets are foretellers and "forth-tellers." It is appropriate for both spiritual and natural fathers to follow these models in working with their children as well.

In bringing up children in the nurture and admonition of the Lord, a father must endeavor to teach God's way and will to his children, both by precept and by example. The prophet Isaiah shows what happens when this kind of godly fathering is put into effect:

All your children shall be taught by the Lord, and great shall be the peace of your children (Isaiah 54:13).

Like the prophets of old, a father must also warn his children. He needs to show them the consequences of their choices and encourage them to make right choices for their lives.

Correct your son, and he will give you rest; yes, he will give delight to your soul (Proverbs 29:17).

A father is responsible for setting an expectation of consistent, godly discipline. Discipline, when administered faithfully and lovingly, provides children with the sense of security that comes when one knows what to expect in every situation.

Train up a child in the way he should go, and when he is old he will not depart from it (Proverbs 22:6).

The very statistics of the state of our children show their need for spiritual fathers. The fatherless generation cries out for discipline, training, and representation to the heavenly Father. It is up to us, the Church, to adopt these young people. Already a move for fatherhood has begun.

Promise-Keeping Fathers

The 1990s ushered in a ministerial movement called Promise Keepers, which inspired men to become followers of Christ through word and deed. It was encouraging to see movements such as Promise Keepers rallying and challenging men to focus on Christ-likeness. Founded by football coach Bill McCartney of the University of Colorado, this nondenominational movement focused on calling men to return to the Father in Heaven.

Thousands of local churches requested information about Promise Keepers, and the organization filled stadiums throughout the country with one million godly men by the year 2000. These men, forever changed, returned to their homes, churches, communities, and careers with renewed purpose and vigor. Movements such as Promise Keepers have helped our families, our churches, our orphaned generation, and our nation return to the heavenly Father.

A Promise Keeper was asked to commit himself to the following godly behaviors:[9]

1. Honoring Jesus Christ through prayer, worship, and obedience to His Word.

2. Pursuing vital relationships with a small group of men, understanding that he needs his brothers to help him keep his promises.

3. Practicing spiritual, moral, ethical, and sexual purity.

4. Building a strong marriage and family through love, protection, and biblical values.

5. Supporting the mission of his church, by

honoring and praying for his pastor and by actively giving his time and resources.

6. Reaching beyond any racial and denominational barriers to demonstrate the power of biblical unity.

7. Influencing his world, being obedient to the Great Commandment (see Mark. 12:30-31) and the Great Commission (see Matt. 28: 19-20).

As *Newsweek* reported in its August 29, 1994, issue, "The movement's message to men is simple: following Jesus is not for women only, nor is it a spectator sport."[10]

As we father this generation, our society will change, America will change, the Church will change, and the family will change. *My prayer is that the fatherless generation will become known as the generation of the Father.*

In Unity With the Father

Jesus prayed, "That they all may be one, as You, Father, are in Me, and I in You; that they also may be one in Us, that the world may believe that You sent Me" (John 17:21). Jesus was in total unity with His Father. He wants us to experience this same unity with Him and with all fellow believers. Such unity is possible, and I believe this prayer of Jesus is being answered in our time.

The bond that a father cultivates with his son is a strong bond of unity that can never be severed if it consists of love, trust, commitment, and prayer. Such bonding is absolutely essential if our society is to survive.

We can learn a great deal from a poignant story a famous author of an earlier century shared about his relationship with his earthly father. One day when he was a boy, James Boswell (the famous biographer of Samuel Johnson) was invited to go on a fishing trip with his dad. After the day of fishing, he wrote in his diary, "Went fishing with my father. The greatest day of my life!"

Years later, after his father's death, Boswell looked into his dad's diary to read his entry for the same day: "Went fishing with my son. A day wasted!"[11]

The elder Boswell had forgotten what it felt like to be a boy. He did not see the importance of building a strong relationship with his son. He had not understood how important the fishing trip was to James.

Fathers in our land today often fail to see the importance of their fatherhood role. Having no relationship with their Father in Heaven, many have not been equipped to build strong, positive relationships with their sons. May God help men in our society reestablish their priorities by putting Him first and following His example in being a father to the fatherless.

Endnotes

1.   U.S. Census Bureau, "Poverty: 2007 Highlights," http://www.census.gov/hhes/www/poverty/poverty07/pov07hi.html (accessed January 2, 2009).

2.   Douglas J. Besharov and Karen E. Gardiner, "Trends in Sexual Behavior," *Amercian Enterprise Institute for Policy Research*,

http://www.aei.org/publications/pubID.17757/pub_detail.asp (accessed January 2, 2009).

3. "Abortions in the United States: Statistics and Trends," http://www.nrlc.org/ABORTION/facts/abortionstats.html (accessed January 2, 2009).

4. United States Advisory Board on Child Abuse and Neglect (1990 Report).

5. "Majority of Children Living with Two Biological Parents," *U.S. Census Bureau News,* February 20, 2008, http://www.census .gov/Press-Release/www/releases/archives/ children/011507.html (accessed January 2, 2009).

6. "U.S. Divorce Statistics," www.divorcemag.com/statistics/ statsUS.shtml (accessed February 21, 2009).

7. Patrick F. Fagan and Robert Rector, "The Effects of Divorce on America," *The Heritage Foundation Backgrounder,* June 5, 2005.

8. Urie Bronfenbrenner, "Discovering What Families Can Do," in David Blakenhorn, Steve Bayme and Jean Bethke Elshtain, eds., *Rebuilding the Nest: A New Commitment to the American Family* (Manticore Pub, 1991).

9. "Seven Promises of a Promise Keeper," http://www .promisekeepers.org/about/7promises (accessed January 2, 2009).

10. Kenneth L. Woodward, "The Gospel of Guyhood," *Newsweek Magazine,* August 29, 1994.

11. Gordon MacDonald, *The Effective Father* (Carol Stream, IL: Living Books/Tyndale House, 1983), 247.

CHAPTER 8

Identity Crisis

Therefore, if anyone is in Christ, he is a new creation;
old things have passed away; behold, all things have
become new (2 Corinthians 5:17).

Who Am I?

Everyone seems to be going through an identity crisis. People are asking themselves, "Who am I? Where am I going? What is my purpose? What is the meaning of my life?" It is a question that even the Church is asking.

Instead of choosing to identify with the righteous character of God, the people of this nation—Christians and non-Christians alike—are identifying with the godless trends and morally deficient character of the world.

What is identity? It is the essence of a person, the inner character he or she displays. The Bible teaches us that we reflect what we see and expose ourselves to. What we put into our spirits—our inner man—is what we will reflect to the world. When we put things into our thought lives that are not of God, it is impossible to reflect God's holiness and His character. As a result, we reflect fleshly weakness instead of manifesting God's power.

> *For as he thinks in his heart, so is he* (Proverbs 23:7a).

Individuals, the Church, and the nation are in an identity crisis. This confusion and emotional and mental havoc comes from our inability to make prudent choices and to establish proper priorities. The only answer is in a relationship with God through Jesus Christ. When we make Him the center of our lives, He gives us purpose and identity.

A Center for Order

Every cell in the human body has a nucleus. All the activity of this cell revolves around the nucleus. Our solar system has a nucleus too—the sun. All the planets revolve in a set order around it. In both cases, the nucleus, or the center, maintains order and prevents chaos.

For example, if a human cell becomes cancerous, its nucleus can no longer maintain order. The health of the entire body is affected by it. Likewise, if the sun no longer maintained the gravitational order for the solar system, the planets would be catapulted into chaos.

The natural tendency of the universe is to degenerate into chaos—a process called *entropy*. A force or nucleus must be present to keep the order. Ultimately, God is the divine force that brings order to life. He is the true nucleus of all that exists. His Son Jesus Christ, the Giver of life, is the only One who can bring peace in the midst of chaos to an individual, family, community, society, or nation. He is the Prince of Peace.

When God is our highest priority, we receive His hope, purpose, and victory. Areas in chaos and disarray then come into proper order. Conversely, when we neglect to put the Lord on the throne of our hearts—in the center of our lives—then lives of disorder, confusion, and defeat result. We walk in the fears and insecurities of the flesh instead of in the confidence of the Lord. Peace escapes our hearts; confusion sets in; and our souls are unsatisfied.

Isaiah wrote, "You will keep him in perfect peace, whose mind is stayed on You..." (Isa. 26:3). God promises that if we identify with Him, He will give us the peace that passes all understanding (see Phil. 4:7). If we don't, the longing of our souls will not be fulfilled. So, in short, identifying with Christ prevents an identity crisis.

When we are in proper order with our center, the Lord God, He becomes our Protector. He acts as a shield to us in all areas of our lives—physically, mentally, emotionally, and spiritually. Our obedience keeps us under His protective covering. When that covering is lacking or is breached because of our disobedience, we can expect to find ourselves in an identity crisis.

This no-direction generation has walked out from underneath the covering of the Lord. Men and women have turned away from their Father, thus finding themselves in an identity crisis. Consequently, children have been left to their own vain imaginations for discipline and guidance.

Men and Women in Crisis

Today men and women face identity crises regarding their gender, sexual orientation, and roles in life. Men have no comprehension or understanding of how to be fathers; women cry out for some Christ-like men within the Church.

Many husbands abuse their wives and fathers abuse their children because they have lost control of their own lives. They have no idea who they are. They themselves grew up in the way their children are being raised—without godly male role models. Left to their own devices and insecurities, they usually manifest anger—sometimes violent anger. Covering up deep-rooted problems, men lash out at their wives, girlfriends, children, employers, and anyone else who may be standing around. They don't want anyone to see that they really are insecure.

Women also, in their identity crisis, can become abusive. Without a sense of godly womanhood, these individuals are left to flounder without direction.

Many of the young people we work with tell us that their mothers abused and neglected them—either physically, mentally, or emotionally. I remember one 14- or 15-year-old boy I saw weeping in the streets. I sat down beside him and asked, "Don't your parents care about you?" His response almost broke my heart. "My dad's not around. He left when I was young. My mom says she loves me, but she had to make a choice because her boyfriend told her that it had to be me or him. My mom picked him and kicked me out of the house."

Unfortunately, this is not an isolated incident. I asked one 15-year-old girl what her parents thought about her selling her body to men on the streets. She replied, "They don't give a damn.

My mom beats me." Another girl said, "You see these marks on the back of my legs? My mother used to take cigarettes and burn them on my leg to punish me."

Women were never called to be the disciplinarian of the home. That is not part of their identity. Women were not called to be both father and mother—and neither are men. God's design is to have both parents partner together in nurturing the family. Together they are to communicate and cooperate as one in the Lord. But when people have no sense of identity, they cannot act according to the character God planned.

Results of the Crisis

Homosexuality is an obvious result of the identity crisis. Because many men cannot conform to the world's "macho" ideal of what a man should be, they become confused. The enemy then comes in, distorts their image of what a man should be, and renders them vulnerable to seduction. God, however, wants each man to look to Jesus as the example of what a man should be. He wants us to identify with His character and spirit. Then men can bear the fruit of His life in all their relationships and responsibilities.

I often have the opportunity to minister to young men who have surrendered their lives to Christ after being active homosexuals. Recently I told one group that some of them had been going through an identity crisis for most of their lives. I explained that their view of what it meant to be a man had become distorted because men and fathers had failed to present consistent godly role modeling in their lives. The examples these young men had been given had not reflected the image of Christ, but the image of the world. They agreed wholeheartedly with me.

A boy's view of other men is formed during early childhood relationships. The outcome of these early relationships may cause a young man to reject the macho image and cling to the male figure who fulfills his needs for intimacy that were not met in childhood. Others may be rejecting a dominant mother figure (usually a woman facing an identity crisis herself) who is trying to be both mother and father in a family.

Men can also seek identity with their friends by going out drinking—neglecting their wives and children at home. When I work out at the gym, I hear other guys boast about their sexual "conquests." They project a very macho attitude. Yet when these same men are with the very women they talk about, they put on an entirely different face—one of insincere, falsely-motivated chivalry. Sooner or later that Dr. Jekyll and Mr. Hyde identity switch catches up with them in a crisis.

Today more women than ever before suffer from a poor self-image as well as sexual confusion. Their identity confusion can be manifested through promiscuity, lesbianism, anorexia, bulimia, and other addictions. Many of these women are rebelling against distorted images and role models in their own lives.

The world may have many terms for dysfunctional behavior, but terms do not bring freedom or provide answers. Jesus provided a way to find true freedom and victory: *Himself.* Until we in the Church focus on true Christ-likeness, this generation will continue to be one in a crisis of identity, ever conforming to society's current status quo. All who do not find their true identity in Christ Jesus will always turn to other things to find purpose and meaning for their lives. Only in Christ will the deepest needs of the soul and spirit be met.

Therefore, if anyone is in Christ, he is a new creation; old things have passed away; behold, all things have become new (2 Corinthians 5:17).

A Nation in Crisis

America as a nation has also walked out from under the Lord's protective covering. We have become sheep without a shepherd, orphans without a father, and people without a purpose. Anarchy fills our hearts, leading us to lawlessness and rebellion.

Our leadership is in confusion. We have allowed a matriarchal spirit—the spirit of Jezebel—to rule over us. Having women in government and leadership positions is not the problem; having individuals with that antichrist, Jezebel spirit in positions of authority is.

In the historical person of Jezebel, we see a very strong personality who was antichrist in spirit. She hated anyone or anything that stood for the holiness and righteousness of God. Whenever anyone tries to quench the voice of truth or to reject God's prophetic voice, that person is operating with an antichrist, Jezebel spirit. This spirit can operate through a male or female. Thus, a woman in a position of leadership who is submitted to her husband and the Lordship of Jesus Christ is not walking in the spirit of Jezebel.

The feminist movement was started by women who did not want anyone to rule over them or to dictate to them what or who they were supposed to be. As they hung on to a root of bitterness, the issue shifted; it is no longer about equality, but about "who gets to rule." Granted, men did oppress women for many years, even in the Church. Men of God should not have been a part of that. Instead, they should have been the ones to lead by example—loving and nurturing the wife and home. If they had, we wouldn't have the problems we do now. The feminist movement was a reaction against those earlier male-chauvinist practices that eventually turned into an overreaction.

A seditious, antichrist, Jezebel spirit—desiring to undermine all that is righteous—rules our nation. When those in leadership—whether men or women—undermine or reject God's constituted authority, they place themselves under the domination of a Jezebel spirit. America is in grave peril. Because the Lord is no longer the nucleus, or the center, the nation is in disarray.

In reality, God needs all of us—men and women—to birth what He wants to do in our generation. For us to have healthy women, we need healthy men who are so secure in their own identities that they are not threatened by the giftings of women. And all of us need to be liberated in Christ.

The New Foundation

In an attempt to disregard the commitment to the Lord in America's foundation, our liberal leaders have laid another foundation—one of mass confusion for the people in this land. Looking for ways to bring national and world peace and harmony without the covering of the Lord, we bring confusion and disorder. When we no longer have a common focal point to maintain true harmony, we actually catapult society into a chaotic search for identity. This search leads people into gangs, cultural barriers, and racial supremacy.

Instead of bringing people together, our leadership has driven them further apart—in political parties, denominations, schools, and homes. Instead of bringing world peace, leaders have actually divided the lines of the peoples of the world.

Consider these words of Jesus:

> *For nation will rise against nation, and kingdom against kingdom. And there will be earthquakes in various places, and there will be famines and troubles. These are the beginnings of sorrows* (Mark 13:8).

In its original text, the word *nation* comes from the root word *ethnos.* It refers to groups of people with common national or racial bonds. It's *ethnicity.* We see many people turning to their ethnic roots in an effort to find out who they are. Racism, ethnocentrism, and sectarianism abound, sometimes in extremes reminiscent of Nazi Germany. This is happening around the world.

Jesus, in describing the end times in this passage, was not just talking about political and international turmoil. He was talking about ethnic and cultural conflicts that would arise between all kinds of groups—racial, ethnic, national, and religious. Such conflicts arise when people are without an identity greater than their own. Harmony and peace will not come to pass without identification with the Prince of Peace.

The moment we enter the Kingdom of God and become His children, we must give up our right to hold on to earthly barriers. We no longer look at the labels, colors, or backgrounds of others. Under the Lordship of Jesus Christ, we are all brothers and sisters. This is the answer to conflict in the world today.

A Christian's first loyalty is not to a cultural background, but to the family of God. That does not mean we should not learn from and take pride in our ancestral heritage; it means that our newfound family in Christ must take precedence. Past oppression, generational hatreds, ethnic struggles—all must be laid at the foot of the cross. The Scriptures tell us that even hating our brother is the same as murder (see 1 John. 3:15). How can we say we love God if we hate our brothers, regardless of their color?

The problems in America and around the country are not an Asian thing, a black thing, a Hispanic thing, or a white thing. It's a misappropriation of identity. God desires to give us an identity in which all of us are the same color—in our hearts. I have an Asian American background, but that no longer matters to me because I am a child of the living God, bought by the blood of Jesus. My first commitment is to the Body of Christ. You see, God transcends beyond all race, culture, and nationality.

We are one family in Christ. His family are those who not only hear the Word of God, but who also do it (see James 1:22). We no longer have the right to cling to our roots of bitterness. Jesus came to set the captives free and to mend the brokenhearted (see Luke 4:18), and we are to follow in His footsteps. In order to do so, we the Church must allow Him to transform us into His image. If we continue to hold on to our own hurts, bitterness, and pains, we will never loose anyone's chains of bondage.

Political leaders, racial leaders, and even religious leaders cannot and will not set this generation free. Jesus can. But we need Him to be our common denominator, the center or nucleus of life. As long as we hold on to our past, we will never move forward into victory. Nation against nation, race against race, culture against culture—this is the by-product of a nation no longer identifying itself with Christ.

We are not of this world; we are of another Kingdom. We need to stop identifying with all the sinfulness and wickedness around us. If we will be transformed to things that are not of this world, God will pour out His anointing upon us.

Yes, there are genuine physical and emotional needs in this stressed-out society. But we are not bound by these struggles! Jesus is the hope set before us.

The search for identity is not a racial thing, a national thing, or a denominational thing. It is a Jesus thing. The true issues in life are spiritual. Ultimately, the quest is a search for the Father.

CHAPTER 9

Nakedness Exposed

Then the eyes of both of them were opened, and they knew that they were naked; and they sewed fig leaves together and made themselves coverings (Genesis 3:7).

Death of Innocence

Adam and Eve innocently enjoyed the fruit and beauty of the Garden of Eden and the companionship of each other until their innocence was destroyed when they ate the fruit of the tree of the knowledge of good and evil. It is the knowledge of evil—in the lives of others, ourselves, and the world—that puts an end to innocence. When innocence is gone, our nakedness is exposed, and we are ashamed.

Innocent children can teach us so much about the good things of life—love, trust, joy, and faith. In many ways, children are able to enjoy most of the fruit of God's Spirit before they lose that innocence: love, peace, joy, patience, meekness, gentleness, faithfulness, and goodness. (Self-control is the exception!)

Jesus said, "Assuredly, I say to you, whoever does not receive the Kingdom of God as a little child will by no means enter it" (Mark. 10:15). A little child has a wonderful capacity to forgive others. He or she is able to trust others as well—that is, until that trust is violated by an adult, which happens in all too many cases in today's society.

Our culture has lost its sense of innocence and purity. It doesn't even seem to value these qualities anymore. The generation known as hippies lived a selfish code even though they proclaimed love and peace. Simply stated, their code was this: "If it feels good, do it." Now parents themselves, the young people of the 1960s are faced with blatant materialism and self-centeredness that tied the 1970s to the 1980s. A major theme of *yuppies*, for example, was, "What's in it for me?" Now we've entered the era of paranoia that seems to be marked by suspicion, distrust, and fear.

We have allowed the standards of this world to mold our identity. If a famous star recommends bisexuality, many reason that it must be OK. If famous male musicians present a feminine image, it must be OK. Comparing ourselves to images portrayed by the media, we are lured into thinking we are inadequate.

In many cases, viewers of television, video games, and motion pictures are led to feel inferior because they believe they do not look as attractive or as alluring. The enemy—a deceiver from the beginning and the accuser of the brethren—delights in bringing people down to his level by making them feel less than adequate.

Somehow he fools people into thinking that having a perfect relationship with the Father will not satisfy them. He whispers, "God the Father will respond to you exactly as your earthly father does." The one whose earthly father is silent, weak, unavailable, unloving, cruel, or neglectful finds it hard to relate to the concept of a loving heavenly Father. Still, this is the deepest need of the human heart.

Two Perspectives

God's Kingdom is one of love, light, truth, and faith. He is perfect love, and He wants His people to know, experience, and enjoy His love. He wants us to take His love and appropriate it in our lives. He wants us to feel His love and to respond to it by loving Him. This is why we were created—to enjoy the love of our Father forever.

Satan, on the other hand, is imperfect in all areas. His is the kingdom of darkness where deception, negativity, distrust, and fear are the prevailing laws of life.

How does satan deceive? Consider this quote from Ed Cole: "Faith is believing that those things you cannot see will come to pass. Fear is believing that those things you cannot see will come to pass." It is the same statement from the perspectives of two totally different kingdoms. You see, satan uses truth with a twisted perspective to deceive. This is exactly what happened in Genesis 3.

Prior to the devil's maneuvers, Adam and Eve were in perfect relationship with God. They were blissfully innocent. They did not know they were naked. If they did, it simply did not matter, for they were incapable of sinning. The lust of the eyes, the lust of the flesh, and the pride of life held no allure for them.

Adam and Eve were so blessed. They had it all—a lush and glorious garden, the joy of the Lord, the peace of God. In fact, they had everything they needed. They were unashamed, truly free, and unabashedly happy.

Then the enemy came. Satan used a biblical truth to convince Adam and Eve that there was something better for them than their already perfect relationship with God. He tempted Eve, "For God knows that in the day you eat of it [the fruit of the tree of the knowledge of good and evil] your eyes will be opened, and you will be like God, knowing good and evil" (Gen. 3:5). Satan was being typically deceitful. He used a truth that said their eyes would be opened and portrayed it as an advantage to be gained. In reality, the only thing Adam and Eve had to gain was evil because what they already had was good.

Isn't that how it is today? Satan deceives people into thinking there is something better than having a relationship with God. Those who believe this lie end up following the devil and his cohorts down dark alleys of sin and degradation.

The only thing we have to gain by seeking the world rather than God is evil. What we sow, we shall reap. If we try to establish our identities according to the standards of the world, we will end up in trouble. I know many people who have greedily reached for all the things that this world has to offer, and they still are miserable. They have no real relationship with those around them. Many think that happiness can be found in bottles, brothels, and barrooms.

Who Told You That You Were Naked?

So when the woman saw that the tree was good for food, that it was pleasant to the eyes, and a tree desirable to make one wise, she took of its fruit and ate. She also gave to her husband with her, and he ate. Then the eyes of both of them

were opened, and they knew that they were na-
ked; and they sewed fig leaves together and made
themselves coverings. And they heard the sound of
the Lord God walking in the garden in the cool
of the day, and Adam and his wife hid themselves
from the presence of the Lord God among the
trees of the garden. Then the Lord God called to
Adam and said to him, "Where are you?" So he
said, "I heard Your voice in the garden, and I
was afraid because I was naked; and I hid
myself." And He said, "Who told you that you
were naked? Have you eaten from the tree of
which I commanded you that you should not
eat?" (Genesis 3:6-11).

Who told Adam and Eve that they were naked? Before Adam
and Eve sinned and gained the knowledge of evil, they were
naked. After they sinned, they were naked. However, they now
looked at themselves with a totally different perspective. They no
longer viewed themselves in purity and innocence, but rather in
shame and embarrassment.

Likewise, who tells us that we are naked? Who tells us that
being in right relationship with God is something to be ashamed
of? Who tells us that we aren't pretty or handsome enough? Who
tells us that we are inadequate? Who tells us that we have to do
certain things in order to be considered acceptable?

It is when we compare ourselves with the world's standards
that we become ashamed of our nakedness. We should not be
ashamed that we have peace that surpasses all understanding. We
should not be embarrassed that we are naked before the Lord

God Almighty. We should be excited that we can walk in purity and innocence before Him.

Their Eyes Were Opened

Adam and Eve's eyes were opened after they ate of the fruit the serpent offered them. They knew they were naked because they gained the capacity to sin.

One of the greatest tragedies in this story about our first ancestors is not that their eyes were opened or that they knew they were naked; it's the fact that their fellowship with their heavenly Father had been violated by their sin and disobedience. It was the end of the only Age of Innocence the world has ever known. This became the inheritance passed down from generation to generation.

Adam and Eve could no longer look at each other in purity and innocence. They also looked upon God with fear. In a sense, their disobedience had rendered them fatherless, at least in the pure and perfect sense in which they had known their Father before. At the very least, their view of God and themselves had been totally marred by sin.

Oddly enough, the world is no longer ashamed of nakedness. Nudity is depicted on all the screens around us. It's difficult to open a magazine, turn on a television set, or go to a motion picture without seeing nudity. Producers and advertisers seem to be ever more daring about projecting such images. Marketing specialists capitalize on the statistic that men and women think about sex several times within a day.

Instead of being ashamed about following the world's standards, we have become ashamed of any degree of openness about

God, beyond "God bless you" and the like. Someone who talks about Jesus is considered to be weird at worst or unsophisticated at best. We are ashamed of righteousness, morality, and taking a stand for goodness. When many people encounter a person who is vocal about his or her relationship with Jesus Christ, they will laugh, mock, snicker, point the finger, or walk away.

Have you ever watched people's reaction when they come upon a Christian witnessing? Those who are at all interested will often cower in the shadows to listen, seemingly hopeful that no one will see them. Some people will make condescending remarks to their companions, as if to suggest that the evangelist is a fool. It's a total reversal of God's plan for His creatures.

Inner Direction

The happiest people on earth are those who love to hear their Father's voice speaking to their hearts. His voice is still and small, but it is very powerful in that it gives them guidance, government, and a sense of security that comes from knowing that they are being guarded by Him. Such people let the integrity of their hearts guide them. Integrity is possible only when one is well-integrated, and such integration comes from an abiding relationship with the heavenly Father. It enables us to make good choices for our lives.

People outside of God's Kingdom, however, do not have such inner direction. Instead, they follow the crowd. It is always interesting to throw out a question to a large assembly of people—a question about how they feel about a particular issue, for example. You will see heads looking all around the room to see who is raising their hands. This happens in Christian congregations as well. Such people let others make up their minds for them. This approach to life always leads to disaster because it is governed by weakness. It makes people very vulnerable to temptation and sin.

The standards of this world are poor guidelines to live by and to make choices by. How could we ever be ashamed of the Father who loved us and gave His Son for us? How could we be ashamed of the Gospel of Jesus Christ, the only power strong enough in the world to save a person from his or her sins? How could we be ashamed of the Lord Jesus Christ who gave His life for us?

Jesus is the One who restores us to righteousness and purity before the Father. This justification by faith enables us to walk and stand in righteousness and complete confidence while in the world. It gives us peace instead of anxiety. The One who is in us is far greater than the one who is in the world (see 1 John 4:4).

Satan has so many people whipped in the world today. They feel worthless, ugly, inferior, ashamed, and condemned. These people have believed his lies. They have compared themselves with the standards of this world instead of biblical values, and they have come up short. When God measures us, He looks upon our hearts, not upon our outward appearance.

> *There is therefore now no condemnation to those who are in Christ Jesus, who do not walk according to the flesh, but according to the Spirit. For the law of the Spirit of life in Christ Jesus has made me free from the law of sin and death* (Romans 8:1).

Combating the Lies of the Devil

Many believers fail to realize that our weapons are not carnal, but are mighty to the pulling down of every stronghold the devil erects. The power of God enables us to cast down vain imaginations and every high thing that exalts itself against the knowledge of God, and to bring every thought into captivity to the obedience of Christ. (See Second Corinthians 10:4-5.)

Thoughts come into our minds—the struggles with inadequacy, low self-esteem, or whatever—and tell us, "You're not loved. You're ugly. You're no good. You're not smart enough. You'll never make it." We know these are lies because they go against the knowledge of God. All those lies that torment us in our minds are vain imaginations. We're to cast them down and bring them into captivity to the obedience of Christ. He is the Lord over every lie that satan could ever throw at us.

The world's approach is to figure things out using their mental reasoning powers and critical thinking ability without looking to the Lord. God's way is quite different: "Trust in the Lord with all your heart, and lean not on your own understanding; in all your ways acknowledge Him, and He shall direct your paths" (Prov. 3:5-6).

God specializes in things that are thought to be impossible. Satan tempts us to think that some situations are hopelessly impossible. When this happens, we forget that our enemy is a liar—the father of lies, in fact—and so we grow discouraged and jump back on the human track of trying to figure things out. At such times, we need to remind ourselves, "God can do anything but fail." He is a miracle-working God who "is able to do exceedingly abundantly above all that we ask or think, according to the power that works in us" (Eph. 3:20).

Our job is to bring every thought captive to Christ, to obey Him in every area. The same power that raised Jesus from the dead is available to us today. That resurrection power is found in the Holy Spirit; He enables us to overcome the things of this world. He renews our minds through the Word of God.

The Giver of Every Good and Perfect Gift

James calls God "the Father of lights with whom there is no variation or shadow of turning" (James 1:17). Our God never changes. He is the same yesterday, today, and forever. He is our Father, and He loves us. He wants to bless us.

> *If you then, being evil, know how to give good gifts to your children, how much more will your Father who is in heaven give good things to those who ask Him* (Matthew 7:11).

Why would anyone deliberately turn from such a loving Father? Why has our generation done so? They have been deceived—and they need to know the truth about our existence.

When we begin to gaze upon the tree of the knowledge of good and evil, when we look to what we don't have, we start wishing we had it. When we don't abide in Jesus, we allow the media's images of slender bodies, beautiful faces, fast cars, and rich lifestyles to flood our thoughts. Our thoughts take on an evil perspective and eventually turn into action.

Certain television programming allows even Christians to invite drug dealers and pimps into their homes. Soap operas and talk shows, for the sake of getting viewers, make abnormal behaviors seem socially acceptable. Married men and women flirt with people who are not their spouses. Often they end up having extramarital affairs because they convince themselves there is someone better. People go into tremendous debt trying to acquire things they want but can't afford. It is a challenge for us to go after what we are not allowed to have. That's the seduction of this world.

Many Christians are being seduced by the false values and philosophies of our world. They want what they should not have. They forget that Adam and Eve ate the fruit they should not have eaten, reaping a harvest of sin and shame. They lost their purity and their innocence and were ashamed of their nakedness before God. They lost their perfect relationship with Him as well—all as the result of going after something they should not have had.

Some believers partake of the same tree that Adam and Eve went for. They find themselves in compromising situations. Sometimes they go all the way back to the world instead of running to God for forgiveness. Their harvest is one of misery, frustration, defeat, and pain.

I had to learn these truths the hard way. Deep within, it seems I always knew that Jesus Christ was the Son of God. I wanted to serve Him, but I often worried that if I surrendered everything, He would send me to Zimbabwe or Borneo or some other far-off region of the world. Such thoughts scared me. I failed to see that they were lies from the enemy.

I wanted to be a "normal Christian." I wanted a wife, a few children, a house with a white picket fence, a nice car, and a fat bank account. But all the while, I knew that God had something more radical for me. Now I know what it was, but then I was scared of it.

As I look back on my life now, I realize that there was nothing to be frightened of. The years of toil and hard work that were focused on getting things were years of frustration and turmoil. They left me feeling unfulfilled and empty. I wanted it my way. God would be part of my life, but on my terms. That simply did not work.

Sensing that I knew what the problem was, I decided, "I'm finished with *my* way. Now I am going to try it *God's* way." When I changed my point of view about my life and my relationship with my heavenly Father, everything began to change for me. Pleasing the world and its citizens meant nothing to me from then on. I discovered that I could experience fulfillment without the acquisition of material things. From then on, all my satisfaction came from serving God.

What a lesson it was for me. God has given me the grace to apply the same approach to my ministry. It has to be done God's way or no way at all. A ministry is not likely to be acceptable to the world. The important question is: is it acceptable to God?

Instead of reaching for the fruit on the tree of the knowledge of good and evil—instead of following the world's standards—reach for the knowledge of God. As we seek Him and His righteousness, all other things will fall into place.

Breaking the Death Cycle

God told Adam that if he ate of the tree of the knowledge of good and evil, he would surely die (see Gen. 2:17). What was He talking about? The death process begins when we partake of the things of the world. Adam and Eve did not immediately die physically, but the process of death began. That process included a spiritual death, which is separation from God.

We can get so used to sin that we don't recognize it as sin any longer. First a thought enters the mind. When entertained, that thought then goes into the heart or spirit.

Sooner or later, it gives place to sin. The death process starts.

When temptations come, we play with it. We think we can get away with sinning before God because we don't experience His judgment immediately. So we believe we can continue in it. The writer of Hebrews frankly shows the error of such thinking:

> *For if we sin willfully after we have received the knowledge of the truth, there no longer remains a sacrifice for sins* (Hebrews 10:26).

The Spirit of grace and the blood of Jesus must not be trampled underfoot. God's Spirit will not always strive with us.

> *For the wages of sin is death, but the gift of God is eternal life in Christ Jesus our Lord* (Romans 6:23).

After Adam and Eve ate the fruit, became aware of their nakedness, and tried to hide from God, they were banished from the garden and from His presence. The divinely appointed cherubim were required to do guard duty, to make sure that the couple would not return to the garden.

Thousands of years later, the second Adam, the Lord Jesus Christ, came in the flesh to redeem fallen humanity. He was beaten, mocked, and crucified. He poured out His blood in order to redeem us, to buy us back from the enemy who had held us hostage.

Now the Son of God invites us to re-enter the garden of God's presence. "I have redeemed you. Come on back into the garden!" We are living in a spiritual garden of Eden. We can walk in a relationship with God today in the spirit realm. This is the ability to walk in peace, joy, excitement, and anticipation of our relationship with Jesus Christ that no man can take from us. We are not kept out of the garden anymore—we do not have to live under the curse anymore!

We are born in the blood of Jesus. We're from another Kingdom now. We do not belong here, although we live here. So we shouldn't be ashamed of the Gospel of Jesus Christ. We shouldn't be ashamed of our nakedness before God and His ability to see right through us and know every part of our lives. He will cover us in His presence if only we would let Him.

Who told us that we were naked? Who told us that we were to be ashamed of what we represent? We should not be ashamed of who we are or the way we look. We no longer need to eat of the lies of this world. We have the righteousness, purity, and holiness of God!

> *Stand fast therefore in the liberty by which Christ has made us free, and do not be entangled again with a yoke of bondage* (Galatians 5:1).

CHAPTER 10

The Spirit of Adoption

For as many as are led by the Spirit of God, these are sons of God. For you did not receive the spirit of bondage again to fear, but you received the Spirit of adoption by whom we cry out, "Abba, Father" (Romans 8:14-15).

God's Adoption

God wants to pour out His heart to this fatherless generation. He *wants* to be a father to a generation that has been misguided and misdirected and overwhelmed by a sense of hopelessness. His invitation has been given; His arms are open and extended to *us*.

Yet how can a generation that has not experienced the love of an earthly father comprehend the love of the heavenly Father? How can we truly understand that Jesus loves us when we do not know that our Father loves us? How can the purity and holiness of God's love be understood when the "love" of earthly fathers has become warped and abusive?

We all—young and old alike—need a revelation of who God the Father is. Our perception of what it means to be a true son or daughter needs to be adjusted. Who will show us the truth about fathers and children? The Holy Spirit, the Spirit of truth, has come to "turn the hearts of the fathers to the children, and the hearts of the children to their fathers..." (Mal. 4:6). It is He who brings the revelation—if we allow Him—that we are the children of God.

> *The Spirit Himself bears witness with our spirit that we are children of God, and if children, then heirs—heirs of God and joint heirs with Christ, if indeed we suffer with Him, that we may also be glorified together* (Romans 8:16-17).

The third member of the Trinity, the Holy Spirit, is known by many different names. He is called, just to name a few: the Spirit of truth, the Spirit of glory, the Spirit of holiness, the Spirit of love, the Helper, the Comforter, and the Spirit of God. He is also called "the Spirit of adoption."

> *For you did not receive the spirit of bondage again to fear, but you received the Spirit of adoption by whom we cry out, "Abba, Father"* (Romans 8:15).

Part of the work of the Holy Spirit, the Spirit of adoption, is to seal us as God's very own (see Eph. 1:13). He verifies and confirms to our own spirits that we have truly received Jesus into our hearts and consequently are *His children*.

As the Spirit of adoption bears witness in our hearts to this change in our lives, we begin to enter into a new and spiritual father/child relationship with God. Now, this relationship is not patterned or molded after our past. It is not modeled on any warped or abusive relationship we may have had in this world. No, this relationship is totally new, and it is patterned after the perfect and unconditional love of the heavenly Father. If you will allow Him to, the Holy Spirit will reveal this relationship to you despite your past experiences.

Although we are not the natural-born children of God, He has chosen us to be His own. We did not choose Him; He chose us. "You did not choose Me, but I chose you..." (John. 15:16).

When the realization that God has chosen you to be His child fully dawns upon your spirit, your life will never be the same. Out of that relationship, you begin to call God "Abba."

Originally *abba* was a word spoken in only a very intimate and close relationship with one's father. In this relationship there is a mutual sharing, a closeness, a bond that nothing can break. Much like a baby lifting his arms for his father to pick him up and embrace him, the word *abba* pictures tender closeness. It's like the words *Daddy* and *Papa* used today.

Because of what Jesus did on the cross, we can approach God not as a starchy, distant "Holy God," but intimately as our "Daddy" whom we love and trust. This is the Father whom our fatherless generation needs to know and love!

Our View of God

So many things in the Church and society have colored our perspective of who God is. Our understanding of God as the

Father is affected by our experiences with our earthly fathers. Few people really understand what a father is supposed to be. Even fewer realize what a godly father is. Some people did not even *have* a father. Many fathers have been abusive or even "absent"—spending more time with the television than with their children.

So many young people in America today grow up without a father figure. Can we blame them for not understanding the heavenly Father? People view God as a mean umpire—grouchy and authoritative—one eager to *call them out*. Others see Him as a rigid disciplinarian, ready with a baseball bat.

Thank God, He is not anything like that. In actuality He says, "If you will listen to Me, I will seal you with My Spirit of adoption. You will be a joint heir through Christ. You will no longer be an orphan, but My child." God seals us by His Spirit.

God desires an intimate relationship with His children. Through this intimacy, God can shape our view of Him and our view of how we think He sees us. We will begin to realize our high value to God. We can experience the depth of His unconditional love for us.

With that kind of confidence, we can go boldly into His presence, addressing Him with the intimate "Abba, Father." We can enjoy the knowledge that He will hear us, speak to us, and meet our needs.

> *Now this is the confidence that we have in Him, that if we ask anything according to His will, He hears us. And if we know that He hears us, whatever we ask, we know that we have the petitions that we have asked of Him* (1 John 5:14-15).

Adopted Heirs

An heir is entitled to receive the estate of his or her father. Adopted children, along with their natural-born siblings, are entitled to share in the inheritance. It is the same way in God's family.

The Father wants us to take on the attitude of *sonship*, of heirs. We are heirs to His character and nature. He transforms us, as we totally surrender to His will and to the Lordship of Jesus Christ, into the image of Christ. His ways become our ways; His thoughts become our thoughts. He gives us the confidence to overcome the wounds, hurts, and wrong choices from the past. He gives us the ability to make the right decisions for the future, to stand for righteousness, and to do His will. He establishes deep roots of His character in us so we can radiate the life and character of God to others.

When we are sealed as the adopted children of God, when we have that stamp of approval by the work of the cross and the Spirit of adoption upon our lives, we should radiate the life of God! People should see a radical difference in our lives. People should know! A person's born-again experience is verified by the radiance of the Holy Spirit upon that individual's life, pointing to the work of the cross. We prove that the seal of adoption is on our lives when we are zealous, transparent, and bold enough to openly let God live in us!

In America

Because the creation itself also will be delivered from the bondage of corruption into the glorious liberty of the children of God (Romans 8:21).

Corruption also means "decay." We see a nation, a generation, in decay. But will they see the glorious liberty of Jesus living in the children of God, in those who have been sealed by the Spirit of adoption?

Not all people professing to be Christian walk in the intimate relationship with "Abba, Father." Romans 9:6 says, "But it is not that the word of God has taken no effect. For they are not all Israel who are of Israel." In other words, not all people who happen to be American are Christian. Billy Sunday said, "Going to church doesn't make you a Christian any more than going to a garage makes you a car!" More than 80 percent of our population claims to have had the born-again experience. But not everyone who says he or she is a Christian is sealed by the Spirit of adoption.

God's love for a generation that has little or no understanding of fatherhood is tremendous! He wants to heal and restore them from all the hurt and abuse. He wants to be the one who gives direction to their lives. But He won't force them to love Him. He'll wait for them to choose the Spirit of adoption.

In the Father's House

> *Even to them I will give in My house and within My walls a place and a name better than that of sons and daughters; I will give them an everlasting name that shall not be cut off* (Isaiah 56:5).

When the Spirit of adoption seals us as God's children, we become something better than being a normal earthly child. He is saying, "What you get with Me is better than anything you could fathom or understand." His care and nurture are better than what an earthly father provides. In short, the intimate relationship we have with God as "Abba, Father" is far greater than any relationship we could have with our earthly parents.

This is the way of the Spirit. When we truly have the Spirit of adoption sealing us, we can walk in God's divine power and nature. We've escaped the corruptions of the world.

Jesus demonstrated this intimate, personal relationship with the Father while on earth. In the Garden of Gethsemane, before He went to the cross, Jesus got on His knees and began to weep before God. He did not say, "O Thou holy Father in eternal ages . . . take this cup from Me." No, He cried out to His Father. As a Son, He bared His soul and heart in openness, vulnerability, and honesty. (See Luke 22:42.)

In the same way, as a child sealed by the Spirit of adoption, you can boldly go into the Father's presence openly and honestly, with assurance of His acceptance. He will speak truth in love to direct you through all your fears and insecurities. You are not approaching a distant father, but a heavenly Father who gave His life for His children. All you have to do is surrender to Him. He has done everything else.

Too many right now are going through so much because they have no idea how *much* God loves and cares for them. God loved us enough that Jesus died for us. He loves us enough to discipline us and to separate us from our sins so that we might experience more of His love, more of His peace, more of *Him*. Even when He disciplines or chastises us, He does so out of love.

> *For whom the Lord loves He chastens, and scourges every son whom He receives. If you*

endure chastening, God deals with you as with sons; for what son is there whom a father does not chasten (Hebrews 12:6-7).

You may have never experienced such complete love on earth, but it is waiting for you with the Father. It is available, if only you will seek it (see Jer. 29:13).

I'll Be Your Father

A few years ago, I went to a meeting that was being conducted by Edwin Cole in Dallas, Texas. Ben Kinchlow, one of the speakers, asked the fathers and sons who were present to come to the front and pray together. As I witnessed this, I began to weep. I had never really had a healthy father/son relationship with my own father. I never learned how to golf, ski, or swim; I never had anyone show me how to do hobbies. I wept because I had never really experienced what it meant to have a daddy, a papa, someone into whose lap I could crawl and not be rejected. I didn't have that father to say to me, "Son, I love you. Talk to me. Tell me what is bothering you."

All of a sudden, as I was weeping, the Holy Spirit spoke to me. "I'll be your Father. I have a desire to be a Father to the fatherless. I will teach you what a father is to be like. I will be your Father. Is there anything you would like to do? I will help you. I will give you wisdom. I will give you instruction. I will give you discipline. I will do hobbies with you. I'll teach you to swim if you want to learn. I'll teach you to snow ski and water ski and to do all these things."

In my mind I questioned, "How can this be? How can God

do those things for me? Maybe He means that He will bring earthly men of God who will be like fathers to me, but that is still not the same."

The Spirit spoke back to me, "No. I will be your Father. I have heard your cry, 'Abba, Father.' You will be My son, and I will be your Father."

By the next year, I had gone snow skiing for the first time. I'm sure I looked like an idiot, but I didn't care because Daddy was with me. I went deep sea fishing for the first time when I was in Australia, and I caught the biggest fish in the group. I even went water skiing, not knowing how to swim, and had a wonderful time with my life jacket on. Daddy was with me. While in Australia, I also went golfing for the first time. I did a lot of "worm burning," hitting the ball across the ground rather than in the air. I also hit the same kangaroo twice, but Daddy was with me.

As I look back on that time, I realized that God was teaching me what it was like to be a son. He was teaching me what it was like to have a daddy who cared—no matter what struggles, faults, insecurities, and pressures I had. He said, "Forget all that and just get alone with Me."

The Spirit of adoption through Christ has made a way for healing and understanding in a wonderful relationship with our Creator, our "Abba, Father." Through the Spirit of adoption, we come under God's divine care and nurture, which includes His discipline and chastisement. He wants us to be the best we can be, like any other parent. He wants to be a perfect father to us so that we might ever be filled with His eternal joy.

CHAPTER 11

Home at Last

When home is ruled according to God's Word, angels might be asked to stay with us, and they would not find themselves out of their element.

— CHARLES HADDON SPURGEON

The Breakdown of the Family

The single most important unit within society is the family. The godly home is the cornerstone of a nation that honors the Lord. The story of Ahab and Jezebel is an example of how an entire nation can be affected by the breakdown of a single home and family. How much more, then, is society affected by the breakdown of untold millions of homes?

King Ahab and Queen Jezebel ruled Israel for 22 years from their palace in Samaria. Their reign took place between 918-897 B.C. Their story is told in the Books of First and Second Kings, and I believe it serves as a prophetic warning to America today— a nation of broken homes and families.

The breakdown of this royal family began with its head, the father, King Ahab. Ahab had a knowledge of God, but no "fear of the Lord." True fear, or reverence and respect, of God always results in obedience to God. Ahab *knew* what was right in God's eyes, but did not *do* what was right.

King Ahab's lack of a fear of God started the disintegration of his family and home. In his resulting disobedience, he became "unequally yoked" to Jezebel, a Sidonian Baal-worshiper. Jezebel was a very strong personality governed by an antichrist spirit. She hated anyone or anything that stood for the holiness or righteousness of God. Ahab, on the other hand, was a weak, double-minded man who took every opportunity to rationalize and excuse himself from doing the will of God. These factors, combined with others, produced a family that knew no fear of God and so abandoned His order for authority and leadership.

Ahab, instead of doing what he knew was right, gave the reigns of the kingdom God had placed in his hands to his strong-willed wife. Too weak to make the proper stand for God's righteousness, he found it easier to let his wife make all the decisions and assume the pressures of responsibility. In this way, Ahab rationalized away the will of God for his own life, his family, and his nation. Although he was called the king, he was little more than a figurehead as Queen Jezebel gladly usurped the God-given authority that should have been her husband's.

The Word of God shows us time and again that if we abandon God's order of authority in the home, the family, the Church, and the nation, *deception* always follows. Ahab became deceived as he went along with his wife's requests to persecute the prophets of God and to destroy any righteous standard in society. He permitted his wife to overrule him, thus completely undermining God's constituted authority in the nation. The children of Ahab and Jezebel had truly become fatherless. Their lack of a father caused the misdirection, desperation, rebellion, and lawlessness that resulted.

This degeneration, which began in the lives of Ahab and Jezebel, continued in their children, and then spread to society as a whole. The breakdown of the family in our society follows the same frightening course. All too frequently, it begins with fathers abdicating their God-given responsibilities, surrendering them to their wives (and even sometimes to their children), thereby, influencing society in a self-destructive course that leads to lawlessness and rebellion.

Ahab turned from God by not fulfilling the responsibilities given him. His son Ahaziah, like his father before him, also turned from God. Ahaziah, though, not only denied the fear of the Lord but even grew up to hate the things of God. With the royal family so corrupted, the nation of Israel could not take a stand for righteousness either. The people can go only so far as the leadership will take them.

A Disturbing Parallel

There is a frightening parallel between this story and our society today. So many in authority are undermining God's constituted authority—forsaking God's ways in favor of their own. In the spirit of Jezebel, they seek to silence the prophetic voices of God to this generation and to quench all those who would stand for righteousness. Their ultimate goal is to destroy any righteous influence in the nation that would challenge their own idolatrous ways. In the spirit of Ahab, we also have leaders who know of God's truths; yet, for the sake of political power and personal comfort, they bow to the dominating Jezebel spirit.

Through all this, today's government rulers place themselves above all that is called of God or is honored as of God. These political leaders, influenced by these wicked spirits, make *themselves* as God by building a society after their own warped image.

Look at the situation the apostle Paul described when he spoke of the coming of the Lord:

> *Let no one deceive you by any means; for that Day will not come unless the falling away comes first, and the man of sin is revealed, the son of perdition, who opposes and exalts himself above all that is called God or that is worshiped, so that he sits as God in the temple of God, showing himself that he is God* (2 Thessalonians 2:3-4).

Could what we have today be the same lawless, antichrist spirit that becomes predominant prior to the Lord's return?

Some leaders in America today will do everything within their power to avoid taking a stand for righteousness, as it is revealed by God in His Word. Although they talk about being Christian, they do not honor the Lord by their lives and actions. Such leaders have embraced the spirits of Ahab and Jezebel. As a result, we have an Ahaziah-like generation, one that mirrors the lawless and ungodly attributes and sentiments of its parents and leadership.

The Ahaziah Generation

It is not surprising that Ahaziah had no father or Father.

His earthly father's weakness blocked him from knowing the power of his heavenly Father. This same phenomenon is happening in our society today. The fatherless generation is the generation of Ahaziah. Our young people are influenced by the spirit of Ahaziah in their approach to worship, leadership, and relationships.

Ahaziah's parents never truly taught him to seek God the Father. Thus Ahaziah turned to the leaders of the world for direction and guidance. He patterned his leadership methods after the idolatrous practices of his society. All standards of God's righteousness were undermined by the "gods" of comfort, convenience, personal ambition, power, and pleasure. Respect for the one true God—the Father of mankind—was nowhere to be seen.

God loved Ahaziah and his fatherless generation however. He loved them enough to send His prophet to warn them and guide them. He was the prophet Elijah, a man of God whom Jezebel had tried to kill. When Ahaziah sought counsel and comfort from the idols of this world, God sent a man whose very name meant "Jehovah is God" to show him his error. God, through Elijah, confronted Ahaziah:

> *Is it because there is no true, living God in Israel that you have gone to seek other gods* (2 Kings 1:6, my paraphrase).

Today God is asking us the same question. "Is it because there is no living God in America and in the Church that you have gone to seek counsel and security from idols, the authority figures, and the resources of this world?" Are not the "securities" of the world *false* securities? Is not the counsel of this world the counsel of the ungodly? (See Psalm 1.) Is not Jesus, the only true God, alive and on the throne of the universe? Why then must we seek other gods—the gods of politics, power, personal ambition, and comfort? On a more personal level, God wants to know, "Is it because you have no relationship with Me through Jesus Christ that you seek the securities of politicians, bank accounts, careers, and other relationships? Is it because there is no righteous standard that you do not seek My heart to find My desire and will for your life?"

America Needs to Return Home

Home is where our Father is. America needs to reestablish the supreme authority of God over the land. As God spoke to the nation of Israel through the prophets He sent, so He is speaking to America today: go home. *The foundation of any nation rests upon the health and the strength of the homes within its borders.* In order for a nation to stand, its home and family structure must be strong.

A family is made up of individuals—you and me. Thus the present deterioration of our nation is the result of, first, the erosion of our own personal relationship with God and, second, the subsequent deterioration of our families and homes. Because we as individuals no longer stand for the righteousness of God according to the covenant we made with Him in and through Jesus Christ, we see the very foundation of our lives and of the life of our nation sinking in the quicksand of moral compromise and hopelessness. With this compromise comes the destruction of all that is godly!

Because we as a nation no longer place our wholehearted love and devotion in the Lord Jesus Christ, we put our affections on the things of this world. Those happen to be the very idols that bring so much suffering, misery, and pain to our children, marriages, relationships, and our very lives. The result is a Church that does not shine any light in the darkness around it. The Church, for all intents and purposes, is so much like the world that it suffers the same problems and seeks the same answers as those to whom it is supposed to minister!

An antichrist spirit is prevalent in this nation. America, a nation that once trusted and placed God at the center of its authority and value system, has left its first love. In place of Christian truth, we have developed our own standards of right and wrong—with some results that make no sense! It's not OK to kill a rat, but it is OK to kill a baby in the womb. It's not OK to read the Bible in school, but it is OK to teach about homosexuality as an alternative lifestyle. It's OK to kill if you have a good reason; a child can divorce his or her parents. The list of travesties is endless.

Instead of repenting, our nation continues to wander aimlessly down the paths of sin and corruption. Very much like Ahaziah, who refused to repent of his sins as they were pointed out by Elijah, we turn against the message and the messenger.

Ahaziah's Response to God

Ahaziah got angry and sought to bring God's ambassador into bondage. In his arrogance, he sent his troops three times to capture Elijah in an effort to silence him. Three times Ahaziah tried to subject God's authority under his own. The soldiers called out to the prophet, "Man of God, the king demands that you come down from the hill." In complete ignorance, they thought they held the sole authority. They soon learned an important lesson: God, and no other, is king! "Thus says the Lord, the King of Israel, and his Redeemer, the Lord of hosts: 'I am the First and I am the Last; besides Me there is no God'" (Isa. 44:6).

> *Then the king sent to him a captain of fifty with his fifty men. So he went up to him; and there he was, sitting on the top of a hill. And he spoke to him: "Man of God, the king has said, 'Come down!'"* (2 Kings 1:9).

The soldiers' emphasis was not on the authority of Elijah as a "man of God." Had they honored God as God, they would not have commanded Elijah, in the name of the king, to "come down" and submit himself to *their* authority. It is quite clear that King Ahaziah's authority was being placed higher than God's authority. It was like this: "I'm the king—the governor, the senator, the president—and you, prophet of God, are going to bow down to me! If you want 'religious freedom,' you have to listen to me!"

How did Elijah respond? Humbly, he said, "If I really *am* a man of God, then may fire come down from heaven and consume you." Now God's consuming fire can either refine and anoint for the accomplishment of His will, or it can burn a person into a "crispy critter." At issue in either one of these alternatives is *the motive of the heart.*

> *So Elijah answered and said to the captain of fifty, "If I am a man of God, then let fire come*

down from heaven and consume you and your
fifty men." And fire came down from heaven and
consumed him and his fifty men (2 Kings 1:10).

It depends on our motivations and on what spiritual garments we wear as to whether that consuming fire burns us in fiery judgment or anoints us to be the witness God has called us to be! The first two groups of soldiers show us the result of arrogantly challenging God's sovereignty.

How I wish the leaders of our nation would learn of God's power and truth. He is the King. Did Ahaziah learn his lesson? No, he held on to his arrogance and his idolatry. He had contempt for Elijah, the bearer of God's warning that came in love. He turned his heart even further away from God, just as our leadership has done. Our government can legislate all that they want, but it will be to no avail. God can bless only the nation that stands for His righteousness and exalts His name!

Ahaziah responded by sending a second contingent of troops to Elijah. Like the first force, these men were consumed by the fire of God. Incredibly, Ahaziah remained defiant, hardhearted, and unyielding. He sent a third regiment to Elijah.

This time, however, the captain came to his senses. He knew what had happened to the others, and he recognized that true authority and power reside in God the Father. In all humility, he fell on his knees before Elijah and pleaded, "Man of God, please let my life and the lives of these fifty men be precious in your sight."

Again, he sent a third captain of fifty with his
fifty men. And the third captain of fifty went up,

and came and fell on his knees before Elijah, and
pleaded with him, and said to him: "Man of
God, please let my life and the life of these fifty
servants of yours be precious in your sight. Look,
fire has come down from heaven and burned up
the first two captains of fifties with their fifties.
But let my life now be precious in your sight"
(2 Kings 1:13-14).

Ahaziah's commanding officer humbled himself before the man who represented God. He acknowledged God's authority as being higher than King Ahaziah's, whom he represented. In essence he was pleading for mercy, and he placed his whole command in submission to God when he presented himself and his men as Elijah's servants.

Our nation's leaders need to come to the same realization that this captain did. They need to realize that no matter what earthly authorities they represent, all must humble themselves before the highest Authority in the universe—out of covenant love, not out of forced subjection. They need to see that our first priority must always be to serve God, not necessarily the kingdoms of the world. This was the spirit in which the founding fathers established America. Our society has deteriorated because the Spirit of God is forgotten.

Ahaziah died in his sin, unrepentant. The same judgment will come to America if we fail to heed the Word of God. Ahab and Jezebel left misery, unhappiness, and shame to their descendants. What will the fatherless generation of today bequeath to its children? The Ahaziah generation was cursed by God because they would not submit to God in a covenant of love. What will happen to us? We can learn from Ahaziah; indeed, we must learn in order to stave off the curse of the Lord.

The Power of Prayer

We can learn another important lesson from Jehoram, Ahaziah's brother, who took over the kingdom upon Ahaziah's death.

> *Now Jehoram the son of Ahab became king over Israel at Samaria in the eighteenth year of Jehoshaphat king of Judah, and reigned twelve years. And he did evil in the sight of the Lord, but not like his father and mother* [it would be hard for anyone to match that degree of wickedness!]; *for he put away the sacred pillar of Baal that his father had made. Nevertheless he persisted in the sins of Jeroboam the son of Nebat, who had made Israel to sin; he did not depart from them* (2 Kings 3:1-3).

The Scriptures go on to say that Moab rebelled from under Israel's domination. Jehoram, afraid that Moab might one day gather forces to invade Israel, decided to wage a campaign designed to bring Moab back under subjection to his rule. Now at that time the kingdom of Israel was divided. Because of Solomon's previous disobedience to God, God split the kingdom of Israel into the kingdoms of Judah and Israel. Each kingdom had its own king and was at odds with the other more often than not.

During the reigns of Ahab, Ahaziah, and Jehoram, King Jehoshaphat reigned in Judah. King Jehoshaphat was a good king, a man after God's own heart. However, he had one abiding fault. He desired so much to see the divided kingdom reunited (in heart, if not in actual monarchy) that he was willing to compromise in order to accomplish that feat. His compromise came in the form of unholy alliances, first with King Ahab and then with Ahab's son Jehoram. In First Kings 22, we see that this unholy alliance almost cost Jehoshaphat his life. In Second Chronicles 19, the Lord strongly rebuked Jehoshaphat for his actions. King Jehoshaphat's desire was good, there is no doubt. However, even if our desire is good, it does not justify the compromise of God's commandment in order to accomplish that good. Jehoshaphat failed to see that, although his heart was in the right place, it was not the right *time.* Another King, whose name is Jesus, was and is to be given that task!

Jehoram, knowing Jehoshaphat's heart (see 1 Kings 22:44), enlisted his aid as did his father before him. He said, "Will you go up with me to fight against Moab?" Loyal Jehoshaphat replied, "I will go up; I am as you are, my people as your people, my horses as your horses" (2 Kings 3:7.) In other words, even though Jehoshaphat knew Jehoram hated God, his heart and his vision for a reunited kingdom in submission to God clouded his judgment enough to commit to an "unequal yoke" with the king of Israel. Perhaps he thought he could win Ahab and his sons to the Lord! I don't know. However, I do know that *nothing* justifies the accomplishment of God's will if it means going outside of God's will.

So Jehoram, king of Israel, and Jehoshaphat, king of Judah, along with the king of Edom, journeyed to the land of Moab (see 2 Kings 3:9). In the wilderness of Edom, these three kings became stranded without any water for the hosts following them.

The ungodly cried out in despair. However, King Jehoshaphat sought God for counsel and aid. Jehoram did not even think about seeking God during this crisis. But Jehoshaphat said, "Is there no prophet of the Lord here, that we may inquire of the Lord by him" (2 Kings 3:11). In other words, Jehoshaphat knew where his source was and *did* become that witness to Jehoram that he perhaps desired to be.

When Elisha the prophet was found, Elisha said to Jehoram, "What have I to do with *you?* Go to the prophets of your father and the prophets of your mother" (2 Kings 3:13). In other words, Elisha was saying, "Why are you coming to me? Where are the gods of your mother and father? Let them help you if they can!" Ahab, Jezebel, and Ahaziah had repeatedly tried to capture and kill Elijah, Elisha's mentor. Now we see Jehoram coming to that same spiritual resource for help. Then as well as now, God continues to show the world that there is *help* only in Him!

Here is my primary point in the account of Jehoram warring against the Moabites. In Second Kings 3:14, Elisha says, "As the Lord of hosts lives, before whom I stand, *surely were it not that I regard the presence of Jehoshaphat king of Judah, I would not look at you, nor see you."* Elisha says quite clearly, "Jehoram, I'm not going to honor your request. However, because *Jehoshaphat* is here, a man who is in covenant with the Lord God of Israel, because *he* is inquiring of me, I will come to your aid and seek God on your behalf."

Pray!

America faces enemies, both natural and spiritual. Our leaders have in large part abandoned God. They rely on our military and economic strength, forgetting that it is God who has blessed us and protected us in the past.

America needs more than a "Jehoshaphat" now. We need total repentance and revival if we want to stay God's judgment. Unless we wake up, our light will be taken from us. We need to *pray* for our land. We need to pray for our President, that he submit to the righteousness of God and the will of God. When he does, he can then truly lead us—lead us back to the heart America had when God first founded and established this nation. We need to pray that our President will not be like Ahab, Ahaziah, or Jehoram, but will be courageous and humble enough to admit any error and stand for the righteousness that he knows he should!

In the midst of all that God is about to do in this nation, I believe there will be revival—revival of a remnant. We need to be ready for it. *We need to proclaim to a desperate, discouraged, and misdirected generation that the only living and true God is alive and among us—if only we will reach out, take His hand, and work with Him!*

CHAPTER 12

The Days of Noah

And as it was in the days of Noah, so it will be also in the days of the Son of Man: they ate, they drank, they married wives, they were given in marriage, until the day that Noah entered the ark, and the flood came and destroyed them all. Likewise as it was also in the days of Lot, but on the day that Lot went out of Sodom it rained fire and brimstone from heaven and destroyed them all. Even so will it be in the day when the Son of Man is revealed (Luke 17:26-30).

Total Denial

People in Noah's day refused to believe his prophetic message. They denied and avoided the truth at all costs, ignoring the reality of God's inevitable judgment of sin.

In the same way, people in our society deny and ignore Jesus' warning:

> *"Whoever seeks to save his life will lose it, and whoever loses his life will preserve it. I tell you, in that night there will be two men in one bed:*

the one will be taken and the other will be left.
Two women will be grinding together: the one
will be taken and the other left. Two men will be
in the field: the one will be taken and the other
left." And they answered and said to Him,
"Where, Lord?" So He said to them, "Wherever
the body is, there the eagles will be gathered
together" (Luke 17:33-37).

We are living in a day when human, spiritual, and natural disasters are accelerating. Tsunamis, earthquakes, hurricanes, famine, wars, genocide, AIDS virus—the headlines every day tell a grim story.

And you will hear of wars and rumors of wars....
For nation will rise against nation, and kingdom
against kingdom. And there will be famines,
pestilences, and earthquakes in various places.
All these are the beginning of sorrows. Then they
will deliver you up to tribulation and kill you,
and you will be hated by all nations for My
name's sake. And then many will be offended,
will betray one another, and will hate one an-
other. Then many false prophets will rise up and
deceive many. And because lawlessness will
abound, the love of many will grow cold. But he
who endures to the end shall be saved (Matthew
24:6-13).

Although Jesus told us that no man knows the exact day or

hour, He said that there are signs to help us know that the hour of redemption is drawing closer. These signs are becoming ever more apparent today.

Enemies of the State

Jesus said that people would hate believers, that they would be offended by us, and that they would even kill us. While this once seemed unthinkable in the United States, we are now living in a time when Christians are reviled by many in this nation. Christians are called homophobic, hate-mongers, intolerant, etc. Many even consider Christians to be this nation's greatest enemy!

To believe that Christians are a detriment to society is a deception. How can someone with deep moral convictions be a danger to society? The extremes to which some individuals go to denounce Christians as hate-mongers fulfill the Scripture that says a time will come when good is considered evil and evil is considered good (see Isa. 5:20).

How can we find truth when things are so twisted around? Jesus said we will know people by their fruits (see Matt. 7:16). Are things done from love or from spite? I cannot speak for all Christians, but in the circles I walk in, we do not hate those who disagree with us.

In one situation, where pro-choice activists were harassing pro-lifers, a man confronted me. He said, "I hate you! I hate your God!" He then proceeded to curse the name of Jesus. As I walked across the street, I looked back at him and said, "If I was in the street bleeding to death, you would laugh and mock me to scorn. If you were in the street bleeding to death, it's my kind of people who would try to help you." Which one of these was an act of love?

At one of our Friday Night Alive meetings, a handful of members of Queer Nation came to challenge me. They called me a Christian bigot, a hatemonger, and a number of other derogatory names. One of them, a disc jockey, challenged me to debate a former member of the Gay Political Caucus on his radio program. I refused. Weeks later, however, I was on a Christian call-in talk show, and this same man called to challenge me. I turned the conversation back on him by asking, "Where were all your true friends when you needed help?" I told him that our ministry had found out that he had a personal financial need, and unbeknownst to him, we had paid his electric bill. I told him that we had been keeping him in prayer. God honored our witness of love. Days before this man died from AIDS, he accepted Jesus Christ as his personal Savior.

A true Christian is never an "enemy of society." The fact is, many of us came out of lifestyles in which we *were* a hindrance and a threat to society. Many of the members of our ministry used to be drug addicts, alcoholics, criminals, homosexuals, prostitutes, and otherwise lawless individuals. The Lord Jesus Christ, though, has transformed them into people He can use. Though once they had no convictions or respect for human life, they are now people of purpose, compassion, and love. Formerly fatherless, they have learned that newness of life comes through submission to the true Father in Heaven. Now they themselves reach out to others. For example, many minister to people who are HIV-positive. Others visit shut-ins and prisoners. Some volunteer to help troubled youths and gang members. Such people are not enemies of the state; they are the salt of the earth.

Actions Speak Louder

Monica, one of my spiritual daughters, tells people that it was my encouragement that helped bring to birth her ability to recognize her value and purpose, thus pushing her into her destiny. She was broken and angry when I met her at one of my Bible studies in the 1990s. She said:

> I didn't really trust men, and I never had a father. Doug taught me what it was like to have a spiritual father, but most of all he taught me how to receive my Abba Father. He loved me in spite of my anger and hurts and brought healing to me because he truly accepted me as a daughter. I am the woman I am today because of his father-heart.

By providing a spiritual family and home to those in a Fatherless society, we can lead them to their true place of refuge—a relationship with their heavenly Father. The Church must become the spiritual families to this orphaned generation so they might see the love of Christ in us, which will point them to our heavenly Father.

Truth has become distorted in our society today. We need to share the truths of God's Word with this generation so the truth will set them free. They need to know that God is their Father and that Jesus, the Truth, is the only way to Him.

Who Is the Father?

Through the centuries, great leaders and their nations have turned from the Father. From Nero to Napoleon, from Hitler to

Saddam Hussein, these people have turned their backs on the very answer to their needs. Jeremiah points out that those who turn their backs on God receive the same treatment from the Father (see Jer. 18:13-17). Our leaders are in danger of following the footsteps of all these ungodly empires. He will turn His back on us if we continue to walk in idolatry and sin. We need to return to the Father, the Almighty God. As we do, we need to recognize Him in each of the following attributes and give Him Lordship in each area.

God is *Yahweh* and *Jehovah.* These Hebrew names mean "the Lord," the governor and ruler over all of the universe. Who is the Lord of our lives? Who rules on the throne of our hearts? Many of the problems in society today stem from our pride and self-centeredness, from our need to be our own rulers.

God is *Jehovah Elohim,* "the Lord is God." He is the ever-present God who always is. He is the real God; all other gods are false idols. To worship any other is idolatry.

As *Jehovah Elyon,* He is "the Lord God Most High." As our Father God, He is high above all that we know and could ever consider. We cannot conceive of His grandeur, glory, and might. However, our unclean society needs to give Him the honor due Him.

El Shaddai is the Almighty God. No one is greater. No one is more powerful. How exciting to think that the One in whom all power and authority reside has determined to live within the hearts of all who love Him. No other leader or authority figure can match the power of our Father.

God is also *Jehovah Jireh,* the Lord who will provide. He promises to supply all our needs. Government, no matter how hard it tries, cannot provide everything for its people. We cannot look to our political leaders as our suppliers.

Our loving Father is *Jehovah Ropheka,* which means "the Lord is our Healer." He binds up the brokenhearted, sets the captive free, heals the lame, and gives sight to the blind. All healing comes from Him. This sick and dying fatherless generation needs the power of the Lord who heals.

"The Lord is our righteousness;" He is *Jehovah Tsidkenu.* All in our society need their filthy rags exchanged for His righteousness. No one is truly good without Him. We need His righteousness imputed to us through His Son in order to be able to keep His laws of goodness and holiness.

Jehovah Nissi is "God the Conqueror." Satan is a defeated foe; the battle is already won. It is Jehovah Nissi who gives us the victory over sin, self, sorrow, and satan; He sets us free from enslavements and addictions that rob us of our freedom.

"God is our peace;" He is *Jehovah Shalom.* Let us raise this banner for all of the world to see. There can be no peace without Him. Until hearts find the cure of restlessness in the Father, they can have no lasting peace.

Finally, God is *Jehovah Shammah,* "the Lord is there." He is with us; we can lean on Him. He won't leave us or forsake us (see Heb. 13:5). With God as a "very present help" (see Ps. 46:1), there is no reason for us to be afraid.

This fatherless generation needs to know that the Father is there for them in every way. When the fatherless find their Father, all the blessings that God wants to bestow will fall into place. Our only hope for America—for families, children, homes, churches, society—is for this generation to come to the Father. A generation with an intimate relationship with God will do mighty exploits for Him. Let's be willing to show them the way.

Building for the Next Generation

I was privileged to know the late Rick Husband and his wife Evelyn. Rick was an astronaut and the commander of the Space Shuttle Columbia for its 28th mission. He invited me to speak at a reception taking place just prior to the launch of the Columbia in January of 2003. At the reception, Christian music singer Steve Green sang Rick's favorite song, "God of Wonders." The words to the song say, "God of wonders, beyond our galaxy...." NASA would play this song for Rick to wake him up while he was in space. Can you imagine waking up and looking out the window of the Space Shuttle at the galaxy and hearing those words?

Rick had wanted to be an astronaut his entire life. He loved his work, but he knew that even more important was his life beyond the space program. He measured his success by being a good husband and father and as an example for Christ on the job and in everything he did. One of my spiritual fathers, the late Dr. Edwin Louis Cole, founder of the Christian Men's Network, used to say, "Christ-likeness and manhood are synonymous." Rick Husband learned this principle in his life.

Leaving a Legacy for the Next Generation

One of the things that impressed me so much about Rick was when I found out that each day he would have a devotional time with his son and his daughter. For the 2003 Shuttle mission, Rick knew he would be gone sixteen days and so, not wanting to miss his devotions with his children, he prepared sixteen video messages for them to watch—one for each day he would be in space. On the sixteenth day, his children put in the last video and got to spend one last video devotion with their dad, excited for his return home.

Of course, we know the tragedy of that day, as the Space Shuttle Columbia disintegrated over East Texas during re-entry into the Earth's atmosphere. Rick and the rest of the seven-member crew did not make it home that day. But the life that Rick Husband lived before he entered the portals of eternity influenced the generation to come. We never know when our moment will come, but we must always sow to the future.

Rick Husband was a man whose life foundation was solid, built on the principles of God's Word. His commitment to the Lord was steadfast, and his family was secure on the rock foundation of Christ, even after he left this life for the next.

Looking for Something to Believe In

The next generation wants something to believe in. They want something they can give their lives for. They want to know heroes like Rick Husband, who inspire them to live their lives with purpose and dedication.

Heroes of the faith are willing to risk their own lives to rescue the perishing at all cost. Every generation needs heroes—men and women we can look up to and emulate. The Bible is filled with stories of heroic believers who obeyed God and did mighty exploits in difficult situations. We are told to consider their faith and imitate their manner of life. The writer of Hebrews makes several references to those who should be imitated:

> *We do not want you to become lazy, but to **imitate** those who through faith and patience inherit what has been promised* (Hebrews 6:12).

> *Remember your leaders, who spoke the word of God to you. Consider the outcome of their way of life and **imitate** their faith* (Hebrews 13:7).

> *Let us fix our eyes on Jesus, the author and perfecter (or finisher) of our faith, who for the joy set before Him endured the cross, scorning its shame, and sat down at the right hand of the throne of God. **Consider Him** who endured such opposition from sinful men, so that you will not grow weary and lose heart* (Hebrews 12:2-3).

Not finding positive heroes to imitate, many of our young people today have sadly latched onto negative heroes. From perverse rock stars, gang leaders, television stars, and athletes, the list goes on. Many destructive role models have substituted for the heroes our generation so desperately need. Just as the Bible points to heroes of the faith whose example we should follow, it also gives many warnings about imitating the ways of evildoers:

> *Do not be misled: "Bad company corrupts good character"* (1 Corinthians 15:33).

> *Dear friend, do not imitate what is evil but what is good. Anyone who does what is good is from God. Anyone who does what is evil has not seen God* (3 John. 1:11).

> *Blessed is the man who does not walk in the counsel of the wicked (ungodly) or stand in the way of sinners or sit in the seat of mockers. But his delight is in the law of the Lord, and on his law he meditates day and night* (Psalm 1:1-2).

> *When you enter the land the Lord your God is giving you, do not learn to imitate the detestable ways of the nations (peoples) there* (Deuteronomy 18:9).

Lives Worth Imitating

Years ago, NBA basketball star Charles Barkley stirred quite a controversy by insisting that he not be considered a role model. He argued that no one should imitate him just because he was a sports star. Charles Barkley's effort to distance himself from sainthood is perhaps understandable. He has never claimed to be a model of spirituality, and he doesn't want anyone to expect that of him. What he failed to see, however, is that those in the public eye have an inherent impact on their fans and society around them. We as Christians, or should I say those who claim to follow Christ, should be concerned when we try to make the same argument.

While it is true that we certainly aren't perfect—and won't be anytime soon—that is no excuse to shrug off our responsibilities to reflect the love and character of Christ. If our Christian life is so hypocritical and compromised that it isn't worth imitating, we need to take serious review of our lives. Leonard Ravenhill used to say, "Are the things you're living for, worth Christ dying for?"

The apostle Paul had no reluctance to challenge people to follow his example. Not in a self-righteous manner, but with a spirit of humility and with confidence he could say:

> *Follow my example, as I follow the example of Christ* (1 Corinthians 11:1).

> *For you yourselves know how you ought to follow our example . . .* (2 Thessalonians 3:7).

> *Even though you have ten thousand teachers (guardians) in Christ, you do not have many fathers, for in Christ Jesus I became your father through the gospel. Therefore, I urge you to imitate me* (1 Corinthians 4:15-16).

> *But you have carefully followed my doctrine, manner of life, purpose, faith, longsuffering, love, perseverance, afflictions . . .* (2 Timothy 3:10-11).

I don't think Paul challenged people to imitate him because he was some kind of super-Christian. But he knew that with a clear conscience, empowered by the grace of God and a posture of humility, he could confidently say that the life of Christ in him was worth imitating. God is not looking for clones of modern-day Christianity but imitators of Christ.

Dr. Edwin Louis Cole often said that "Champions are not those who never fail but those who never quit." We need a persevering spirit because we need winners and champions for Jesus. We need modern-day heroes of faith and courage.

It's a sad fact that many of today's young people are not impressed by the examples set before them. We have not been heroic in our fight against spiritual darkness in our land, but rather have often been seduced by it. Try as we might to encourage others to be zealous disciples of Christ, it is hard for them to accept our message when it is undercut by our complacent and uninspiring lives.

Paul encouraged both Christians and unbelievers to follow his example. King Agrippa asked Paul, "Do you think that in such a short time you can persuade me to be a Christian?" Paul's reply was great: *"Short time or long—I pray God that not only you but all who are listening to me today may become what I am..."* (Acts 26:28-29).

If we are honest, we will have to admit that today's Church has often been a laughingstock in the eyes of the world. We have provided fodder for comedians and talk-show hosts to ridicule the Gospel. A healthy respect for the things of God is replaced with a yawn or a chuckle.

The story has been told of a Sunday school teacher who asked the children in her class, as they were on their way to the church service, "And why is it necessary to be quiet in church?" One bright little girl replied, "Because people are sleeping!" It is time for us to awaken from our sleep and arise!

Someone once suggested that we should include the following songs to our hymnals:

- A Comfy Mattress Is Our God

- My Hope is Built on Nothing Much

- Be Thou My Hobby

- Pillow of Ages, Fluffed for Me

- I Surrender Some

- I'm Fairly Certain That My Redeemer Lives

- Sit Up, Sit Up for Jesus

- What an Acquaintance We Have in Jesus

- Take My Life and Let Me Be

A Church that is soft and apathetic will never succeed in reaching a lost and hurting world. People, young people in particular, will be reluctant to give their lives for something that is shallow and hypocritical. Even unbelievers and the unchurched are tired of the hype and pretense. They are looking for reality and for something to believe in. They won't be moved with anything less. They are the **hope of the future**, a prophetic generation just ready to come forth into their destinies.

Home Is Where You Start From

There is a saying, "Home is Where You Start From." This is precisely what the fatherless generation needs. God has a prophetic destiny for this generation, but He is looking for mothers and fathers in the faith who will establish a strong foundation for the next generation to build upon. God is looking for His people to be a launching point for the emerging generation of youth, that we might bless and release them into their God-given destinies.

During the cultural revolution of the 1960s, a great rift occurred between the generations. One of the era's mottos was, "Don't trust anyone over 30." A generation was seduced away from their fathers (and mothers)—and even more importantly, away from their Heavenly Father. The enemy's plan was to have a generation estranged from both spiritual and moral authority. His plan has largely worked, and for the last 40 years we have seen the consequences of that estrangement.

However, God is doing a mighty work in our day! In Malachi 4:5-6, there is a prophetic promise of a great coming together of the generations before the Lord's return.

> *Behold, I am going to send you Elijah the prophet before the coming of the great and terrible day of the Lord. He will restore the hearts of the fathers to their children and the hearts of the children to their fathers, so that I will not come and smite the land with a curse.*

Could it be that we will begin to see the fulfillment of this promise in our day? Is now the time for the hearts of the children to come back home? We must ask ourselves then, will we have a home for them to return to? Will we build a strong foundation that will become a refuge for them from the storm?

The Time Is Now

The time is now to awaken from our slumber and begin building a strong foundation for the next generation. We must heed the storm warnings and determine that no longer on our watch will the fatherless be abandoned. No longer will the orphans be without hope. We cannot sit by and watch the statistics become worse. Christ is the answer, and we possess that answer. As He lives in us, we must become the answer for the fatherless generation.

Let us return to the moral and spiritual foundations upon which our nation was established—the foundation of God's Word. Let us make building strong families our priority, in order that our communities, our churches, and our nation may be strong. Let us align ourselves to the principles of God's Word so that our course will be straight.

The time to build is now. Storms will come, of this we can be sure. But on the rock foundation of Christ, the rains and floods and winds will not be able to cause us to fall.

> *"And the rain fell, and the floods came, and the winds blew and slammed against that house; and yet it did not fall..."* (Matthew 7:25).

In my earlier book *Who Will Cross the Jordan?* I discussed many of the factors that influence the fatherless generation. In it I called our present generation "the no-direction generation." Little by little, God began to reveal to me the reason our current generation suffers from a lack of direction. It is because they do not have a Father.

Those of this fatherless generation, like the Israelites of old, wander aimlessly in a wilderness of confusion and darkness. They cannot find their way into the Promised Land. It is our responsibility to lead and guide them back to their Father in Heaven.

Pumping through our spiritual veins is the blood of Jesus. Our spirits pulsate with the presence of the living God. How can we possibly fail in our mission to the fatherless generation with such spiritual resources available to us?

May our prayers be like this prayer/poem given by Leonard Ravenhill to his sons more than 30 years ago:

Give Me a Son
(Author Unknown)

*Build me a son, oh Lord, who will be strong enough
    to know
When he is weak and knows enough to face himself
    when he is afraid
Who will be proud and unbending in honest defeat
    and humble and gentle in victory
Build me a son whose wishbone will not be where his
    backbone should be*

*A son who will know Thee—and to know himself as
    the foundation stone of knowledge*
Lead him I pray, not in the path of ease and comfort
*But under the stress and spur of difficulties and
    challenge*
Here let him learn to stand up in the storm
Here let him learn compassion for those who fail
Build me a son whose heart will be clear
Whose goal will be high
*A son who will master himself before he seeks to
    master other men*
One who will learn to laugh yet never forget to weep
*One who will reach into the future, yet never forget
    the past*
*And after all these are his, add I pray enough of a
    sense of humor*
*So that he may always be serious yet never take
    himself too seriously*
*Give him humility so that he may always remember
    the simplicity of true greatness*
*The open mind of true wisdom, the meekness of true
    strength*
*Then I, his father, will dare to whisper:
    "I have not lived in vain."*

Somebody Cares America/International

Somebody Cares America/International operates in local communities across the United States. and internationally, bringing hope by meeting the day-to-day needs of individuals in personal crises and by mobilizing our existing network of ministries to respond to global tragedies.

Your ongoing prayers and support enable us to be the hands and feet of Jesus in the midst of daily need—physical, emotional, and spiritual—in our communities, throughout the nation, and around the world.

Because Jesus cares, we care. And because you care, lives across the globe are impacted daily.

Thank you for caring!

FOR MORE INFORMATION OR A LIST OF
SOMEBODY CARES CHAPTERS, CONTACT:

SOMEBODY CARES AMERICA
P.O. BOX 570007
HOUSTON, TX 77257-0007
713-621-1498

somebodycares@somebodycares.org
www.somebodycares.org
www.dougstringer.com

Additional copies of this book and other
book titles from DESTINY IMAGE are
available at your local bookstore.

Call toll-free: 1-800-722-6774.

Send a request for a catalog to:

Destiny Image® Publishers, Inc.
P.O. Box 310
Shippensburg, PA 17257-0310

*"Speaking to the Purposes of God for This
Generation and for the Generations to Come."*

For a complete list of our titles,
visit us at www.destinyimage.com.